The Transcendental
Meditation Program
for Business People

An AMA Management Briefing

The Transcendental Meditation Program for Business People

ROBERT B. KORY

53287

amacom

A Division of American Management Associations

World Plan, Science of Creative Intelligence, SCI, Transcendental Meditation, and TM are the service marks of the World Plan Executive Council in the United States.

Library of Congress Cataloging in Publication Data

Kory, Robert B
   The transcendental meditation program for business
people.

   (An AMA management briefing)
   Bibliography: p.
   1. Transcendental Meditation. 2. Executive ability.
I. Title. II. Series: American Management Associa-
tions. An AMA management briefing.
BL627.K67   294   76-3696
ISBN 0-8144-2189-X

This Management Briefing has been distributed to all members enrolled in the Personnel Division of the American Management Associations. A limited supply of extra copies is available at $5.00 a copy for AMA members, $7.50 for nonmembers.

First Printing

53287

Contents

About the Author

ROBERT BRUCE KORY is a summa cum laude graduate of Yale University with a degree in philosophy. While an undergraduate, he became interested in the Science of Creative Intelligence (SCI) and its practical aspect, the Transcendental Meditation (TM) program. After completing a teacher-training course conducted in 1971 by Maharishi Mahesh Yogi, the founder of SCI and the TM program, he became a qualified instructor of the TM program and SCI.

Mr. Kory has served as chairman of the center for the Transcendental Meditation program in Hartford, Connecticut. In Hartford, at the Institute of Living, he worked as an instructor and research assistant for a project investigating the value of the TM program for psychiatric patients. He also directed a research project in the Hartford and East Hartford public schools in which 200 students took a credit course in the Science of Creative Intelligence.

In 1973, Mr. Kory became regional coordinator of the Transcendental Meditation program for the New York Metropolitan area. In that position, he set up symposiums on TM and management in many major U.S. cities.

Currently National Vice-President for Expansion of the American Foundation for the Science of Creative Intelligence, he recently received a large federal grant to investigate the value of SCI for students in six northern New Jersey high schools. Mr. Kory is co-author of the best-selling *TM: Discovering Inner Energy and Overcoming Stress* (Delacorte Press, 1975) and *Happiness: The TM Program, Psychiatry and Enlightenment* (Simon & Schuster, 1976). He is currently finishing a book on the TM program and management.

Preface

Interest in the Transcendental Meditation (TM) program has multiplied geometrically over the past several years. When the first scientific research on the TM program was published in 1970, TM practitioners in the United States numbered less than 30,000. Five years and 200 studies later, nearly one million people are practicing the TM technique in the United States alone. Among the most enthusiastic practitioners are the leaders of many of America's largest corporations.

In the not too distant past, the name "Transcendental Meditation" may have conjured up visions of magic carpets, long-haired yogis sitting on mountain tops, or just plain unrealistic thinking. Scientific research, recent best-sellers on the TM program, and nationwide press and media coverage are rapidly dispelling these misconceptions. The Transcendental Meditation program has nothing to do with flower children or religious cults. In fact, TM is proving to be among the best currently available approaches to improving individual and organizational performance. For this reason, many large and small corporations are introducing in-house TM programs to improve productivity, job satisfaction, employee health, and human relations.

The TM program appears to be a unique method of unlocking human potential in the organization. While other behavioral science techniques attack specific individual or organizational problems, the TM program fosters comprehensive individual growth by expanding individual consciousness. The TM program apparently provides a direct means for the individual to tap deep reserves of energy, intelligence, creativity, and happiness inherent within the machinery of the mind and body. Involving neither group process nor intellectual analysis, the TM program works by means of natural *physiological* processes.

How does the TM program affect individual performance and health? What can a TM program contribute to organization development? What might the TM program mean for the future of business? These questions have guided my efforts in examining the TM program for business in this comprehensive yet summary fashion. Discussion of the Transcendental Meditation technique itself is reserved for Appendix A. I have written this briefing in the hope that people in business might better understand and thereby profit from a new paradigm for progress in their field.

Throughout the manuscript I will be using the terms *TM technique* and *TM program* in two very specific ways. The term TM technique refers to a unique meditation practice taught under the auspices of the educational service divisions of the World Plan Executive Council (for further explanation see Appendix A). The term TM program refers to the twice daily practice of the TM technique and the TM follow-up services, which assure maximum benefit from TM practice.

Because the TM program has become widely known, some people have begun calling their meditation techniques TM and advertising them at "bargain" prices. Their techniques are not TM and have not been scientifically investigated. I would caution the reader at the outset that when discussing how the TM technique works and what the benefits of the TM program are, I am referring to a technique and program taught only by qualified TM instructors through one of the divisions of the TM organization, which is nonprofit and active through 400 offices in the United States and in over 60 countries worldwide.

1
Developing Human Potential in Business

Over the past 30 years, the responsibilities of the personnel manager and function have undergone radical change and expansion. The application of behavioral science techniques to the people problems within profit and nonprofit organizations has demonstrated a fact that no management can overlook. A tremendous untapped potential for improved performance lies dormant in the human resources of virtually every organization. Consequently personnel management no longer means simply hiring and firing and working out job descriptions, wage scales, and employee records. In a growing number of organizations, the personnel manager faces the problems of job satisfaction, motivation, absenteeism, turnover, team building, interpersonal competence, and, ultimately, productivity among his most challenging responsibilities.

To deal successfully with these problems, a number of methods have become prominent. Management by objectives (MBO) has gained widespread recognition as useful in improving employee performance and job satisfaction. Sensitivity training, usually conducted in T-groups, has long offered the promise of unfreezing people and helping them to work together more effectively. Herzberg's motivation studies finally propelled job enrichment to the forefront of approaches to improving performance. Transactional analysis has become popular as one of the latest methods for improving people's abilities to work together.

These approaches to developing human potential in organizations are but four well-known methods among a vast array of techniques that include process analysis, third-party intervention, personnel assessment, and confrontation sessions. Results of all such efforts have contributed to the growing conviction among top management that significant cost reductions and productivity gains may be achieved by freeing the human potentialities that lie in reserve everywhere.

Yet, in reviewing the results of job enrichment and sensitivity training in his organization, a personnel supervisor in a large manufacturing firm told me: "I think the first CEO who read Abraham Maslow opened a Pandora's box. None of the behavioral science methodologies seem to work consistently from company to company, plant to plant, or from person to person in the same plant." The widely acknowledged inconsistent results of behavioral science techniques and the many failures of other techniques pose a challenge to business. The *Work in America* study reports that only 20 percent of the over 100 companies surveyed about the results of job enrichment programs reported even moderate success.[1] Sensitivity training has come under heavy fire over the last several years as only moderately helpful to some people and potentially harmful to others. How to integrate the insights gained during T-group sessions into day-to-day routine appears to be a yet-unsolved problem with sensitivity training.

Does this mean that Maslow, Argyris, Herzberg, Likert, McGregor, and their colleagues have overestimated human potential? Is the idea of developing human potential OK for the university but all wet for business? The fact is that few people dispute the validity of the theories: As early as 1900 the father of American psychology, William James, wrote:

> I have no doubt whatever that most people live, whether physically, intellectually or morally, in a very restricted circle of their potential being. They make use of a very small portion of their possible consciousness, and of their soul's resources in general, much like a man who, out of his whole body organism should get into the habit of using and moving only his little finger.[2]

One quite recent study has come up with an alarmingly low

figure in estimating that most people use little more than 5 to 10 percent of their intellectual, emotional, and physical potential.[3] Furthermore, a number of companies *have* achieved dramatic results in some of their plants using some of the behavioral science techniques currently available. In his book *The Failure of Success*, Alfred J. Marrow has collected reports of how behavioral science techniques have worked in a cross section of American business firms.[4]

Stumbling Blocks to Human Development

If the theories are sound, then why do so many organizations have trouble using behavioral science techniques to develop the potential of their personnel? The common response to this question is that people resist change. Beach and Mahler emphasize the need for two to three years' preparation time in implementing an MBO program in order to overcome "traditional resistance to change by the staff."[5] In introducing new training methods in Detroit Edison, R. E. Schwab reported the need for "special strategies to overcome resistance to change."[6] The *Work in America* study cites resistance to change as the *primary* obstacle to job enrichment efforts.[7]

Most behavioral science techniques currently in use involve interpersonal processes. In MBO, a group tries to set mutually agreeable and reinforcing goals. In sensitivity training, a person learns through group interaction about how he responds to others and how others respond to him. In a job enrichment program a group of managers may work together to redesign the jobs of their subordinates to increase the responsibility content of those jobs. In order for these processes to be effective, members of the group must feel secure enough in themselves to participate in a free give and take about issues of significant personal importance.

The plain fact of organizational life, however, is that very few managers or employees show sufficient psychological flexibility and inner self-assuredness to act and react openly with others about issues in which heavy emotional investments may be at stake. Resistance to facing up to personal insensitivity, hesitancy in becoming committed to measurable objectives, unstated fears of giving up responsibility to subordinates, delay in implementing new training methods, disinterest in understanding interpersonal transactions, and anger at the prospect of third-party intervention are common stumbling blocks to nearly all current techniques.

13

If we can recognize that most people in organizations do not enjoy a state of sufficient psychological well-being and inner happiness to permit openness to change, then we can begin to understand why they have such resistance. When a person lacks a strong baseline experience of inner happiness, he becomes dependent upon the environment for his psychological well-being. Any change in the environmental routine may signal some degree of unconscious threat. The excessive concern which many people show about how others evaluate them and their performance, as well as the all too common angry or defensive responses to criticism, indicates the psychological rigidity prevailing in most organizations.

By contrast, when a person enjoys a high level of baseline happiness, he easily adapts to change. Because he enjoys life in his day-to-day routine, he is not heavily invested in "doing things his way" in order to feel confident that he is moving ahead in the organization. The process of dropping defenses and discovering inner ease and well-being is what sensitivity trainers mean by "unfreezing." Almost anyone who has undergone some degree of unfreezing in a T-group becomes aware of both how frozen most people are and how slowly unfreezing takes place through a group process.

Another reason people resist change is stress. Stress is the body's nonspecific, automatic physiological response to any demand made upon it. A loud noise, a viral infection, or an angry memo from the president all trigger the same physiological processes of the body preparing itself for fight or flight. The demands made on managers in most organizations today tend to trigger the stress response very frequently. Already faced with difficult problems, many managers will perceive the prospect of organizational change as yet another troublesome demand. Anger, defensiveness, anxiety, and an array of emergency emotions often accompany the stress response, reducing mental clarity, clouding judgment, troubling interpersonal relations, and wasting energy.

It would seem, therefore, that an organization requires a means of fostering individual growth *directly* without dependence on group process techniques. If a person could increase his ability to handle stress and directly tap inner reserves of energy, intelligence, creativity, and happiness, improvement in performance, well-being, and interpersonal effectiveness could be expected. One program which has been shown to produce these benefits for the individual is TM. Perhaps because the TM program seems to accomplish this goal while avoiding the stumbling blocks of other organization development strategies, a growing number of companies are exploring the value of the TM program for improving productivity, job satisfaction, employee health, and human relations. By directly enhancing individual strength and well-being, the TM program may soften resistance to other organization development strategies and catalyze teamwork.

The TM Program

Some people may still associate the TM program with magic carpets, "pretzel" positions, or some sort of unrealistic thinking. In fact, the TM program is a systematic means of allowing a person to gain access to his reserves of energy and intelligence while naturally improving physical health and psychological well-being. Research on the physiological, psychological, and sociological effects of the TM program has been completed or is under way at over 200 institutions, including Harvard, UCLA, and Stanford. Studies on the program have been published in major journals all over the world, including *The Academy of Management Journal, The Conference Board Record, The American Journal of Psychiatry, The Journal of the American Medical Association*, and *The Journal of Psychosomatic Medicine*. Organizations exploring the value of Transcendental Meditation include Connecticut General Corporation, Crocker National Bank, American Telephone and Telegraph, Blue Cross–Blue Shield, and the U.S. Army.

As an approach to developing people and organizations, the Transcendental Meditation program has unique features: First, it does not depend upon group process. An individual practices TM by himself. Second, it does not depend upon intellectual analyses of behavior, but works by fostering a natural improvement in the functioning of a person's nervous system.

The TM program complements rather than replaces most of the behavioral science techniques used in organization development. By directly increasing energy, creativity, intelligence, and psychological well-being through improved functioning of the individual nervous system, the TM program fosters the inner stability and happiness people need in order to make group processes work.

Herzberg's motivation studies have shown the incongruity between the real nature of motivation and the carrot and stick practices commonly used in the name of motivating employees. In demonstrating that people are motivated by a self-sustaining inner drive for achievement rather than pay scales and bosses' threats, Herzberg opened a new dimension in organization development. He made it clear that to unlock their potentialities people must be helped to get in touch with their inner drives. They cannot be helped by manipulation from the outside. It's ironic that despite his discovery, nearly all the techniques used in organization development today involve processes which help people get in touch with their personal resources only *indirectly* by way of the group.

The TM program has been called a major scientific discovery because it permits a person to gain *direct* access to untapped inner resources. The main principle underlying growth through the TM program may be stated simply: By increasing the order and integration in the functioning of the nervous system, a person may enrich all aspects of his life. The new science of psychophysiology has established the intimate connection between the functioning of the mind and the functioning of the body. The so-called psychophysiological principle formulated by physiologist Elmer Greene at the Menninger Clinic states that every thought or feeling must involve a corresponding change in bodily functioning. What this means for human development in business is that it may be possible to promote individual growth through a direct physiological approach rather than a psychological one. If a person improves his psychophysiological functioning—that is, if his nervous system begins functioning in a manner that is less inhibitory or wasteful of energy—then he may gain increased access to his full potential.

Physiologist R. K. Wallace, pioneer researcher on the TM program, discusses the progressive integration of the nervous system resulting from the practice of the TM technique in terms of the expansion of consciousness.[8] Because the brain and nervous system control every aspect of a person's life, their improved functioning would be expected to foster improvement in all areas—health, psychological well-being, interpersonal relationships, intelligence, perceptual ability, mind-body coordination, memory, and so on. Expansion of consciousness seems to be the most appropriate term to describe the growth process that accompanies integration of the nervous system through TM practice.

Consciousness may seem to be a somewhat intangible concept in relation to individual performance. In fact, consciousness is the yardstick for measuring potential to perform. Everyday experience illustrates the significance consciousness has for performance. If a person does not get a good night's sleep, the functioning of the brain and nervous system is impaired, resulting in a low level of awareness. Almost everyone understands the costs of this generalized dullness to health, interpersonal relations, clarity, and energy level. On the other hand, when the brain and nervous system are functioning especially well, a person experiences a high level of energy, great mental clarity, a generalized sense of well-being, and robust health. The difference in performance is striking.

The TM program, by permitting a person to improve the functioning of his nervous system in a natural, systematic, and comprehensive manner, expands consciousness. It is therefore a direct means of helping people gain access to their full measure of energy, intelligence, creativity, and psychological well-being.

NOTES

1. *Work in America*, a report of a special task force to the Secretary of Health, Education, and Welfare. Cambridge, Mass.: MIT Press, 1972.
2. W. James, *William James on Psychical Research*, edited by G. Murphy and R. V. Ballou. New York: Viking Press, 1963.
3. F. S. Perls, *Gestalt Therapy Verbatim*. La Fayette, Calif.: Real People Press, 1969.
4. A. J. Marrow, ed., *The Failure of Success*. New York: AMACOM, 1972.
5. D. N. Beach and W. R. Mahler, "Management by Objectives." In *The Failure of Success*, edited by A. J. Marrow. New York: AMACOM, 1972, p. 237.
6. R. E. Schwab, G. M. Worbois, and L. E. Kanous, "How Detroit Edison Built a More Effective Organization," in Marrow, op. cit., p. 314.
7. *Work in America*, op. cit.
8. R. K. Wallace, "The Neurophysiology of Enlightenment," presented at the 26th International Congress of Physiological Sciences, New Delhi, India, 1974. Reprinted New York, Maharishi International University Press, 1974.

2
View from the Top

As will be seen later, scientific research demonstrates several objective benefits of the Transcendental Meditation program. But how does the practice of TM affect the day-to-day routine of people in business? To answer this question, subjective reports are helpful. Before examining the scientific research on the benefits of the TM program, let's take a look at what people in business say about the Transcendental Meditation program. Subjective reports do not constitute scientific proof of what TM does for performance and well-being, but they do help place technical research in a practical perspective.

Business Week quotes Shervert Frazier, professor of psychiatry at Harvard Medical School: "I have seen it [the Transcendental Meditation program] in use and it works.[1] *Industry Week* notes that "Transcendental Meditation is becoming known for its favorable track record . . . ."[2] *Connecticut Business and Industry* writes that most executives who practice TM issue no public statements but agree "that TM has been of immense benefit to them."[3]

Several years ago when TM was still relatively unknown, many prominent executives were reticent to talk about their experiences publicly. They were content to enjoy the benefits and let others discover TM for themselves. Scientific research on the TM program and public acclaim for its benefits have since changed this situation. Taken together, the following interviews offer some initial insight into what the expansion of consciousness through TM practice means for the day-to-day routine of people in business.

Feeling Good

How important is feeling good to productivity? Almost everyone has days when he feels great and other days when he just does not feel at his best. On the good days, even the big problems do not seem unsolvable, but on the bad days, minor problems become disproportionately annoying. Science offers no good quantitative measure of "feeling great," but few people deny that feeling good is an important factor in peak performance. Perhaps the most common benefit which executives report soon after beginning the Transcendental Meditation program is a general improvement in how they feel.

The vice-chairman of a large consumer and prescription products company summarized this single, most comprehensive benefit of the TM program when he told me: "Since starting TM, I feel more energetic and, at the same time, more relaxed. And then there's a feeling that is a little hard to describe: I feel more contented, with feelings of elation which are completely natural. I just feel *good*, if I may use a very simple word."

Hartzel Lebed, senior vice-president at Connecticut General Corporation, participated in the in-house TM program held at the company's home office in Bloomfield, Connecticut. Several months after learning TM, he said: "When I first heard about TM, someone made a statement about everybody having good days when they really feel sharp, creative, and productive, and that TM helps people feel that way all the time. I've never forgotten that statement. I feel that in general this benefit has materialized for me since I've started TM. Maybe not 100 percent, but I really do feel a good deal sharper, more productive, more creative, and more efficient since I've been practicing TM." Theodore Rosky, also a vice-president at Connecticut General, added: "I'm more able to cope with the little nitty-gritty problems that I encounter daily at work since starting TM. I've been enjoying much more ease, much less frustration, and a much better outlook on the future."

Do these improvements in general well-being directly contribute to a person's productivity? A direct correlation may be difficult to establish scientifically, but Joe Namath, another "manager" who tests his skills on Sunday afternoons, summed up how TM and "feeling good" affect performance when he said: "I've enjoyed TM and I'm going to keep on enjoying it. It's a lot more fun being able to go out there and relax and play the game than to go out there all tensed up and afraid you're going to make a mistake. And through TM it happens that way."[4]

Mental Clarity and Emotional Stability

James Sinclair, a general partner in the Wall Street firm Vilas and Hickey and a renowned expert in international finance, reported another difficult-to-measure but profound benefit of the TM program. Our interview proceeded as follows:

Kory: Have you noticed any benefits in your work since you started the Transcendental Meditation program?

Sinclair: Oh, absolutely. From the day I started four years ago, things have improved and they have continued to improve.

Kory: What benefit has been most important to you?

Sinclair: Freedom from environmental conditioning.

Kory: What do you mean by that?

Sinclair: What I mean is freedom from being emotionally moved by and at the mercy of the surrounding circumstances. Without TM, if business is good, you're elated; if business is poor, you're depressed. If circumstances work out the way you want, it's great; if circumstances work out contrary to your desires, you have a difficult time. Freedom from environmental conditioning through TM means ability to handle the situation no matter what happens.

Kory: Isn't that pretty abstract?

Sinclair: Abstract that's not; that's money making! A man who does not emotionally succumb to difficulties at work, who doesn't allow difficulties to structure his thinking and his life, is able to negotiate the difficulty. A man who meets a difficulty at work and begins to feel tense and put the blame on his surroundings is a person about to go out of business. Environmental conditioning impairs judgment, impairs intuition, impairs human relations, impairs the person in every sense. Transcendental Meditation frees people from this conditioning and thereby removes the self-created barriers to success.

21

Mr. Sinclair largely attributes his consistently outstanding investment profits to benefits of the TM program.

The president of one of *Fortune*'s top 50 companies began the TM program just about the time he became president. He noted: "Because of TM, I've been able to take greatly increased responsibility without much stress and strain in an environment which has been very unfavorable to business. This freedom from stress even under pressure has probably made for better decisions. In my position, that's important." Another *Fortune*-top-50 company president, who has practiced TM for 18 months, mentioned a similar benefit. He said: "I think TM has helped me become less emotionally caught up with business problems. As a result, I've got what seems to be a consistently broader perspective on the issues at hand."

Broad awareness and emotional stability contribute to effective decision making. Because the TM program fosters these qualities, executives value taking 20 minutes twice a day to do TM. Although science does not yet offer the tools to measure how this benefit of the TM program may affect productivity, Larry Bowa, all-star shortstop with the Philadelphia Phillies, has a very easy way to measure its effects on his performance. Noting his increased emotional stability and mental clarity in the face of problems, Bowa said: "I know Transcendental Meditation helps me. It takes away tensions and anxieties. I don't let little things bother me anymore. Last year every game I played carried over. I let things build up, and before I knew it I was 0 for 28. I was buried. Now, if I go 0 for 4, I start all over the next day, just like a new season for me. The same with my home life. I used to take things out on my wife, but Transcendental Meditation helps me leave baseball problems at the ball park."[5] Since starting the TM program, Bowa's batting average has jumped from .210 to over .300.

Improved Mental Capabilities

Extensive scientific research indicates that the program improves the functioning of the mind. Some of the research results are presented in Appendix B. Improved problem-solving ability (Chart 12), increased creativity (Charts 18 and 19), more orderly thinking (Charts 11, 12, and 13), and increased intelligence (Chart 9) are all among the effects reported by scientists investigating the TM program. Do people in business note these benefits in their day-to-day lives?

Constantine Anagnostopoulos, general manager of Monsanto's New Enterprise Division, pointed out that "instead of having just one working day, you have almost two of them after starting TM. Specifically, my most productive hours—everybody has his own—have been in the morning from about 9:00 to 11:00. If I have a difficult problem to solve or a difficult report to write, I use 9:00 to 11:00 as the period of my most productive and creative output. I don't really have to do that anymore. After I go home and meditate in the evening and have dinner, I can take 9:00 to 11:00 at night just as well as 9:00 to 11:00 in the morning for even my most difficult work."

Ronald Lee is the northeast regional manager for technical services at Xerox. Since starting TM, he has noted: "I'm much less tired and I have the ability to shift concentration from one particular area of activity to another, almost instantaneously, without getting my previous thoughts caught up with the new problem demanding my attention. I might be talking about a personnel problem on the one hand and pick up the telephone to deal with a marketing problem in the southwestern part of the country. Concentration shifts from one to the other and back again with seemingly 100 percent attention, no effort to remember facts or related issues, no strain to collect my thoughts, and no stress about being interrupted. I am not certain how much of this improvement is attributable directly to TM, but I do find it very rewarding; it must have a positive impact on my productivity."

Michael Gluck is chairman of the Sternberger Motor Company and president of the International Crating and Container Company. He has been practicing TM for about a year. "I don't know whether it's a direct result of TM," he said, "but I think I've been able to approach my work in a more orderly fashion over the past year. I've not only seen a difference in how easily and effectively my own work gets accomplished, but I've organized the management of my corporations in what seems to be a more effective and orderly way as well. Whether or not this is all a by-product of TM, I can't say. But I'm sure TM is a part of it, and to that degree TM has helped my companies."

Physical Health

Another common benefit reported by executives practicing the TM program is improved health. Considerable medical research shows that the TM program reduces psychosomatic complaints and improves resistance to disease. (Because health is a confidential matter, I have omitted names in the following excerpts from interviews.)

A senior vice-president of a large savings and loan association started the TM program because he was suffering from an ulcer and colitis. "I expected TM would help my condition," he said, "but I had no idea I would feel so much clearer at work." A manager at Pratt and Whitney aircraft told me: "I really didn't think TM would relieve my tension headaches. I've tried so many other ways of dealing with these headaches, which always accompany tough days. TM has attacked the problem at its root. My days just don't get that tough anymore."

"I'm no longer taking tranquilizers," a president of a medium-size manufacturing firm told me. "I needed them to control my compulsive eating and nerves. When I told my doctor I was doing TM, he was pleased." A well-known Army general reported that his blood pressure dropped significantly after he started the TM program.

"I save the 40 minutes a day just in my ability to fall asleep quickly and sleep throughout the night," said a top executive with a large manufacturing company. A general partner in a large accounting firm mentioned that he no longer got as many colds as he did before starting the TM program.

The importance of health to peak performance needs little elaboration. Millions of man-hours are lost each year because people are too sick to come to work. Even greater productivity losses result from people coming to work less than fully healthy. The favorable impact of the Transcendental Meditation program on health is not surprising in light of the physiological changes which accompany the practice and which will be discussed in the next section of this book.

Better Human Relations

Business means transactions between people. Many of the problems in business arise because people don't read each other properly. How many mistakes are made because people don't listen? How much energy is lost in defensive reactions to benign situations? How many hours are wasted in sorting out misunderstandings? How much resentment builds up as a result of insensitive supervision? These questions only hint at the scope of the human relations problems of which every manager is aware.

The TM program fosters personality integration, which increases a person's ability to interact effectively with others. Roger Brach is a partner of J. K. Lasser and Company, an accounting firm in New York City. "Since starting TM," he said, "my reaction to stress has changed. In a stressful situation, I no longer get feelings of anxiety in the pit of my stomach. I'm able to deal with problems much more effectively because I am not concentrating on my own emotional reaction to the situation. This benefit has been extremely important to me in my dealings with people. I've noted improvements in my relations with clients as well as other partners in the office."

Michael Fenton, personnel supervisor with AT&T, participated in a small in-house TM program at the Northeastern Long Lines headquarters. He noted: "Within a week after learning the technique, I found that I didn't get annoyed as often when things weren't going exactly as I planned. I seemed to be more tolerant. I expended my energies on getting things done correctly and not on worrying excessively about past problems. Along with higher tolerance came a marked decrease in defensiveness. Psychological tests I took last year showed that I am prone to get defensive when challenged, but I found that since meditating, the aggressive actions of others do not generate defensive feelings as quickly as they used to."[6]

Charles Holman is sales manager for the Connecticut General Insurance Company in the Metropolitan New York area. He added a further insight into how the TM program improves human relations when he told me: "TM helps you roll out of stressful situations quickly and smoothly. For example, when a man comes into your office to discuss a serious personal problem, all the emergency emotions get fired up immediately. Without TM, you might carry that man's problem around with you all day. His problem would get in the way of your relations with everyone else during the day. With TM, on the other hand, this situation disappears. You meet a problem, handle it, bounce back quickly to a baseline feeling of well-being and ease, and are then free to deal with the next situation in the best possible way."

Jay Nichols, president of Nichols Industries, described the effects of the TM program on human relations using some of the language of transactional analysis (TA). "When I get my people to do TM," he said, "it tends to reduce the number of dysfunctional interpersonal games they play. They are getting hooked less (showing fewer inappropriate conditioned responses), and they are not always looking for the crooked psychic reward of playing games. TM seems to strengthen the adult ego states in each of us. You begin to see more clearly what works and what doesn't (calculate probabilities better), and you act accordingly. It also seems to improve individuals' ability to stay in their adult ego state in high stress situations. Transactional analysis offers a good language but no way of directly strengthening the adult getting over games. TM offers a way of directly accomplishing what transactional analysis describes as desirable and normative. TM also appears to strengthen the parent and child ego states with continued practice. It improves an individual's ability to remain in appropriate ego states at appropriate moments."

Summary

Executives report a wide range of benefits from the Transcendental Meditation program. Because people begin the program with different strengths and weaknesses, there are differences in what people report as their most important benefits. Many of these benefits seem hard to measure scientifically and suggest that science may be just beginning to quantify what the expansion of consciousness through TM means for human well-being.

Almost every practitioner of TM agrees that the technique is enjoyable to do. Roger Brach of J. K. Lasser put it this way: "It's not that, at the end of the work day, I feel: 'Oh, gee, now I have to meditate.' Instead, it's 'Great! Now I can take my twenty minutes of TM.'"

NOTES

1. "Personal Business," *Business Week*, October 26, 1974.
2. "Meditation for Managers," *Industry Week*, August 6, 1973.
3. "Business Turns on to TM," *Connecticut Business and Industry*, December 1974.
4. Quoted in Denise Denniston and Peter McWilliams, *The TM Book: How to Enjoy the Rest of Your Life*. Los Angeles: Versemonger Press, 1975. Distributed by Price/Stern/Sloan Inc. (Los Angeles).
5. . Quoted in *Private Excellence in Action*. New York: Maharishi International University Press, 1975.
6. Quoted in *Managers' Forum*, February 1975.

3
View from the Laboratory

During the practice of the Transcendental Meditation technique, the mind effortlessly quiets down to a state of calm inner awareness and the body settles into a state of rest measurably deeper than sleep. A person gains a unique state of consciousness called "restful alertness," which is distinctly different from waking, sleeping, or dreaming. This state cannot be achieved through hypnosis. Neither cat-napping, nor relaxing, nor relaxation exercises, nor biofeedback techniques, nor other techniques which might go by the name of meditation can produce the physiological changes which occur during the practice of TM.

A natural process, the TM technique requires no effort. It does not involve mental manipulation and is not a trance state. A person gains the state of "restful alertness" through the TM technique just as naturally as he wakes up in the morning. A person may have to try to get out of bed, but the process of changing from the sleeping state to the waking state is entirely natural and automatic.

The effects of practicing the program are immediate and cumulative. The reader is again referred to Appendix B for some of the research results. Immediately following 20 minutes of TM, a person may feel increased energy (Chart 17), greater mental clarity (Chart 14), and a sense of well-being. Some of the research[1] indicates that regular practice of the TM technique for 20 minutes twice daily improves learning ability (Chart 10), perceptual-motor performance (Chart 7), and reaction time (Chart 6). Other research shows decreased anxiety (Chart 16), improved ability to handle stress, and decreased use of alcohol, cigarettes, and tranquilizers among regular TM practitioners (Charts 2 and 20). Psychologists indicate that the TM program improves problem-solving ability (Chart 12), increases intelligence (Chart 9), fosters self-actualization (Chart 15), improves memory (Chart 11), and improves concentration (Chart 8). Physicians report that TM seems to reduce insomnia (Chart 4), lower blood pressure (Chart 1), improve resistance to disease (Chart 3), improve asthmatic conditions (Chart 5), and generally reduce psychosomatic diseases.

These effects result from the physiological changes which take place during the practice of TM. The TM program permits a person to gain a state in which body and mind are physiologically *least* excited and *most* orderly. This state of least excitation and maximum order carries over into a person's life outside the 20-minute meditation period. Scientific research on the TM program now fills a 900-page volume. For the purposes of this account, we will limit the discussion to three principal physiological changes which take place during the meditation period: increased orderliness in the electrical activity of the brain, improved balance in the autonomic nervous system, and a sharp decrease in metabolic rate.

TM and the Brain

In the late 1920s, researchers discovered that the brain gives rise to faint electrical impulses called brain waves. Electroencephalography is a technique of recording this electrical activity using electrodes attached to the intact skull and a highly sensitive voltmeter called an electroencephalograph (EEG). EEG research has made significant strides toward correlating specific brain waves with mental-emotional states. Sleep seems to be correlated with 0 to 3 Hz brain wave activity. During relaxation with the eyes closed, 8 to 12 Hz brain waves seem usual, and our normal waking consciousness apparently requires brain wave activity between 13 and 30 Hz.

Electroencephalography is still in its infancy. Nevertheless, recent research on EEG changes during the practice of the Transcendental Meditation technique have shown that the technique produces a unique style of functioning in the brain. When we sit with eyes closed during our normal waking state, brain wave activity measured at one point on the skull shows no general relation to activity at another point. The brain waves are of different frequencies and out of phase. In 1972, Harvard researcher J. P. Banquet discovered that during the practice of the Transcendental Meditation technique, electrical activity of the brain synchronizes.[2] (Figure 1) Banquet reported a synchrony between the front and back of the brain, as well as between the two brain hemispheres. His data also suggest that synchrony may occur between the midbrain (older portions of the brain) and the cortex (the newest portion of the brain). These initial findings have been replicated by several researchers on the TM program around the world and reported in major scientific journals.

The electrical activity of the brain during the practice of the Transcendental Meditation technique becomes more orderly and coherent. The significance of this finding relates to the ways different regions of the brain vary in function. Brain researcher R. W.

Figure 1. Synchrony of electrical activity of the brain hemispheres—Phase coherence.

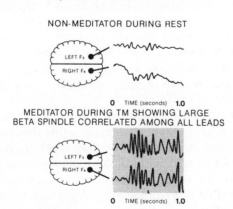

NON-MEDITATOR DURING REST

LEFT F₃
RIGHT F₄

0   TIME (seconds)   1.0

MEDITATOR DURING TM SHOWING LARGE
BETA SPINDLE CORRELATED AMONG ALL LEADS

LEFT F₃
RIGHT F₄

0   TIME (seconds)   1.0

Source: *Fundamentals of Progress*, MIU Press Publication No. U2-16-575, © 1975 Maharishi International University. Research results were originally reported in J-P. Banquet, "EEG and Meditation," *Electroencephalography and Clinical Neurophysiology*, Vol. 33, p. 454, 1972; and in J-P. Banquet, "Spectral Analysis of the EEG in Meditation," op. cit., Vol. 35, pp. 143-151.

Sperry demonstrated that the two brain hemispheres control markedly different mental functions.[3] In general, the dominant hemisphere (left in a righthanded person) is responsible for temporal, linear, analytic, verbal thinking; the nondominant hemisphere (right in a righthanded person) is responsible for imaginative, nonverbal, spatial, holistic thinking. Sperry's research suggests that every person has an artistic and scientific side of his personality built directly into the functions of the two brain hemispheres.

The increased synchronization of EEG activity between brain hemispheres during the Transcendental Meditation technique suggests a physiological basis for the improved verbal ability, intelligence, and creativity seen among people practicing the Transcendental Meditation program. Miskiman, for example, found that TM practitioners show more organized thinking and improved problem-solving ability. This may result from the integration of synthetic and analytic functions. These brain wave changes may also account for improved memory resulting from the TM program.

Canadian neurosurgeon Walter Penfield demonstrated that the front of the brain is primarily responsible for motor performance and the back of the brain for perception.[4] During the practice of the Transcendental Meditation technique, the electrical activity of the front and back of the brain becomes highly synchronous, which suggests that the Transcendental Meditation program might improve perceptual-motor performance. Shaw and Kolb[5] have reported that Transcendental Meditation apparently improves reaction time; Blasdell[6] reported that TM practitioners perform significantly better than nonmeditators on a complex perceptual-motor task. "It sure has improved my tennis" is a frequently expressed comment.

A variety of studies have shown that the midbrain controls our emotions and unconscious bodily processes, while the cortex is the center of thinking and memory. The conflict between emotion and reason—what we know we should do and what we find ourselves doing almost out of compulsion—is as old as man. Some researchers suggest that this conflict arises from lack of integration between the old midbrain and the new cortex.[7] The integration between these two portions of the brain through the Transcendental Meditation program apparently plays an important role in the increased psychological integration and improved sense of well-being among people practicing the technique regularly.

Often people ask whether the same effects of the Transcendental Meditation program might be achieved through just cat-napping, relaxation exercises, biofeedback techniques, or do-it-yourself "meditation" practices picked up from books or magazines. The unique brain wave changes during the Transcendental Meditation technique distinguish the TM program from other practices. Psychiatrist and researcher Bernard Glueck, M.D., reported:

> We have observed a number of individuals who were performing their own variants of meditation, usually a mantra type of meditation, and we do indeed find that they have many changes similar to those seen with the TM meditator. However, these tend to be less consistent and, in terms of the EEG, appear to involve primarily the posterior cortical areas and rarely the frontal areas or the opposite hemisphere. Also, the density of the alpha waves produced is considerably less than that seen with TM meditation. *To date, as observed in our laboratory, TM meditation would seem to produce a maximum effect more rapidly than any of the other techniques.*[8] [Emphasis added.]

TM and the Autonomic Nervous System

The human nervous system is differentiated into two main trunks, the cerebrospinal and the autonomic. The cerebrospinal trunk controls voluntary processes, and the autonomic trunk controls involuntary processes such as digestion, respiration, heartbeat, emotions, and drives. The autonomic nervous system is subdivided into two main branches, the sympathetic (energy-expending) branch and the parasympathetic (energy-restoring) branch.

Ninety-nine percent of the activity in the human body is involuntary and controlled by the autonomic nervous system. Health, energy level, and emotional well-being depend largely on balanced functioning between the energy-expending and energy-restoring branches of the autonomic nervous system. Autonomic balance is so important to health and happiness that physicians differentiate two principal personality types on the basis of the degree of autonomic balance. Stabiles, or people with balanced autonomic functioning, show greater independence, less motor impulsivity, greater resistance to stress, and higher measures of mental health than labiles, or people with autonomic imbalance. Autonomic lability may be a precursor of psychosomatic illness, while autonomic stability is correlated with high levels of resistance to disease.

Medicine has long been searching for a means of increasing autonomic stability. One of the reasons interest in the Transcendental Meditation program has grown so rapidly among physicians is that research suggests that it increases autonomic stability. In 1973, psychologist David Orme-Johnson published the first paper on the Transcendental Meditation program and autonomic stability.[9] He measured galvanic skin responses (the resistance of the skin to a minute electrical current, a measure well known as a lie detector test) among regular practitioners of the Transcendental Meditation technique and a matched control group. Fluctuations in the galvanic skin response (GSR) indicate autonomic instability. In his first study, he compared the number of spontaneous GSRs shown by a group of meditators and nonmeditators while the people sat quietly and comfortably. The meditators showed an average of 10 GSRs over a ten-minute period, while the nonmeditators showed an average of 35 GSRs in the same time period. (Figure 2) Two weeks after the nonmeditators began the Transcendental Meditation program, their spontaneous GSRs dropped to 15 in a ten-minute period. The Transcendental Meditation program apparently improves autonomic stability.

Figure 2. Fewer spontaneous galvanic skin responses.

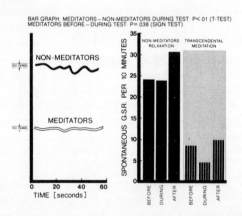

Source: *Fundamentals of Progress*, MIU Press Publication No. U2-16-575, © 1975 Maharishi International University. Research results were originally reported in D. W. Orme-Johnson, "Autonomic Stability and Transcendental Meditation," *Psychosomatic Medicine*, Vol. 35, No. 4, pp. 341–349, July–August 1973.

An important benefit of autonomic stability is increased ability to adapt to stressful circumstances. In his second study, Orme-Johnson tested whether the Transcendental Meditation program contributes to a person's ability to handle stress. The test consisted in measuring galvanic skin responses of meditators and nonmeditators when they were subjected to a sudden noise about as loud as a pneumatic hammer. The noise was delivered over earphones and repeated every half second until the subject ceased showing a galvanic skin response to the noise and had fully adapted to the stress. After 17 repetitions of the noise, regular practitioners of the Transcendental Meditation technique no longer showed a GSR response. A matched control group of nonmeditators continued to show GSRs after 45 repetitions of the noise. Transcendental Meditation significantly increases a person's ability to remain balanced and calm in the face of pressure and stress.

TM, Revitalization, and Purification of the Nervous System

Most psychologists and psychiatrists agree that throughout life people accumulate a backlog of unresolved stresses and strains which remain locked in the nervous system. The body picks up stresses whenever the machinery of the nervous system is subjected to excessive pleasurable or painful stimulation.

The debilitating effects of excess stress on relations with others and on performance, creativity, and health have been well documented. Hans Selye, M.D., the world's foremost authority on the physiology of stress, has identified how people slip into states of chronic tension through the stimulation of the stress response.[10] Chronic tension arises from hyperstimulation of the sympathetic branch of the nervous system without corresponding revitalization of the body through parasympathetic activity. Fatigue, tension headaches, quick temper, insomnia, and gradually rising blood pressure are all signs of chronic stress.

Research on the cumulative effects of exposing the body and mind to deep rest suggests that regular practice of the Transcendental Meditation technique normalizes and purifies the nervous system. During the practice of the Transcendental Meditation technique, oxygen consumption drops twice as much as during the deepest point of sleep. (Figure 3) Biochemical indices of anxiety are removed from the blood four times as rapidly as during sleep. The workload of the heart drops 25 percent (Figure 4), but blood flow to the head and periphery increases significantly. These changes

Figure 3. Change in metabolic rate.

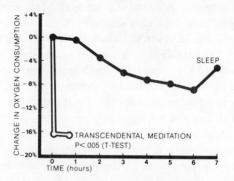

Source: *Fundamentals of Progress*, MIU Press Publication No. U2-16-575, © 1975 Maharishi International University. Research results were originally reported in R. K. Wallace and H. Benson, "The Physiology of Meditation," *Scientific American*, Vol. 226, No. 2, pp. 84–90, February 1972.

Figure 4. Heart rate—Beneficial effects of Transcendental Meditation carried over outside of meditation.

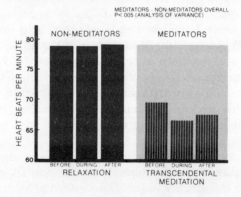

Source: *Fundamentals of Progress*, MIU Press Publication No. U2-16-575, © 1975 Maharishi International University. Research results were originally reported in T. J. Routt, "Low Normal Heart and Respiratory Rates in Practitioners of Transcendental Meditation." Unpublished paper, Huxley College of Environmental Studies, Western Washington State College, Bellingham, Washington.

indicate that the Transcendental Meditation technique produces a unique response in the body which maximizes the energy-restoring and revitalizing activity of the parasympathetic nervous system.[11] These physiological changes account for the energy boost and mental clarity which result immediately from 20 minutes of Transcendental Meditation.

The physiological changes during the technique are the exact opposite of the stress response. The parasympathetic stimulation during the technique apparently neutralizes chronic stress in a natural manner. In addition, the TM program appears to bathe the backlog of unresolved stresses and strains in a state of relaxation deep enough to permit their gradual dissolution. These changes apparently account for the sharp and immediate reduction in anxiety levels among people practicing the TM program. Such changes may also play an important role in meditators' reduced use of alcohol, cigarettes, tranquilizers, and sleeping pills.

The normalization of accumulated stress may also explain the psychological growth which researchers have reported among meditators. Seeman, Nidich, and Banta reported in the *Journal of Counseling Psychology* that the TM program fosters growth in the direction of what Abraham Maslow called self-actualization.[12] They reported increased spontaneity, improved self-assuredness and self-regard, greater acceptance of aggression, and increased capacity for intimate contact among regular practitioners of the TM technique. Other studies have shown that the TM program increases inner control, increases intelligence, decreases anxiety, decreases depression, improves sensitivity to others, and decreases hostility.

It is important to note that these changes do not occur because of any efforts to modify feelings, come to grips with past experiences, or analyze feelings about oneself or others. Psychological growth through the TM program takes place on the basis of physiological changes which occur spontaneously during the meditation period. Because the psychological growth is so natural, meditators often notice these changes only when another person comments on their improved attitudes or behavior.

Summary

The TM technique produces a physiologically unique state of deep rest coupled with heightened mental awareness. This state apparently improves the integrated functioning of the nervous system, increases autonomic stability, reduces chronic stress, and dissolves any backlog of accumulated stresses and strains. These changes account in large measure for the wide range of mental, emotional, and physical benefits resulting from the TM practice.

The physiological changes during TM practice distinguish it from other meditation techniques, cat-napping, hypnosis, biofeedback, and relaxation exercises. The unique brain wave changes which take place indicate that the technique produces much more than simple rest or relaxation. The TM program apparently unfolds a person's full mental potential in addition to reducing accumulated stress. Other meditation techniques do not produce EEG changes equal in magnitude to those which appear during a 20 minute Transcendental Meditation session.

The comprehensive benefits of the TM program result from natural physiological changes in body functioning. Because the program seems to improve every aspect of a person's life, growth through the practice of TM may be described in terms of the expansion of consciousness. This program involves neither group process nor self-analysis, but makes use of the natural laws governing the mind and body to unfold the full potential of the individual in a wholly balanced and spontaneous manner.

NOTES

1. Original papers on all the research mentioned in this section of the briefing are available in the 900-page book *Scientific Research on the Transcendental Meditation Program: Collected Papers*, edited by D. W. Orme-Johnson, L. A. Domash, and J. T. Farrow. Los Angeles: Maharishi International University Press, 1975. This research is also discussed in synoptic form in the best-selling book by Harold H. Bloomfield et. al., *TM: Discovering Inner Energy and Overcoming Stress*. New York: Delacorte Press, 1975.

2. J. P. Banquet, "EEG and Meditation." *Electroencephalography and Clinical Neurophysiology*, Vol. 33, 1972, pp. 449-458.

3. R. W. Sperry, "The Great Cerebral Commisure." *Scientific American*, Vol. 117, 1964, pp. 41–52.

4. W. Penfield and T. Rasmussen, *The Cerebral Cortex of Man: A Clinical Study of Localization of Function*. New York: Macmillan, 1950.

5. R. Shaw and D. Kolb, "One-Point Reaction Time Involving Meditators and Nonmeditators," in Orme-Johnson et al., op. cit.

6. K. Blasdell, "The Effects of Transcendental Meditation upon a Complex Perceptual-Motor Task," in Orme-Johnson et al., op. cit.

7. A. Koestler, *The Ghost in the Machine*. New York: Macmillan, 1967, p. 297.

8. B. C. Glueck and C. F. Stroebel, "The Psychobiology of Transcendental Meditation," in *Current Psychiatric Therapies*. New York: Grune & Stratton, 1975.

9. D. W. Orme-Johnson, "Autonomic Stability and Transcendental Meditation." *Psychosomatic Medicine*, Vol. 35, No. 4, July–August 1973, pp. 341–349.

10. Hans Selye, *The Stress of Life*. New York. McGraw-Hill, 1956.

11. R. K. Wallace and H. Benson, "The Physiology of Meditation." *Scientific American*, Vol. 226, No. 2, February 1972, pp. 84-90.

12. W. S. Seeman, S. Nidich, and T. Banta, "The Influence of Transcendental Meditation on a Measure of Self-Actualization." *Journal of Counseling Psychology*, Vol. 19, No. 3, 1972, pp. 184–187.

4
TM: Productivity,
Job Satisfaction,
and Human Relations

The TM program fosters comprehensive individual growth by improving the functioning of the nervous system. This effect, which cannot be fully grasped by examination of scientific studies alone, is best described in terms of the expansion of consciousness. Ample subjective reports from executives practicing the TM program offer some insights into how the expansion of consciousness affects performance in business. Nevertheless, neither scientific research nor subjective reports satisfy the hardheaded behavioral scientist who wants to know how the TM program relates to practical problems such as productivity, job satisfaction, and turnover.

A pioneer investigator of the TM program in business, David Frew, Ph.D., began studying the effect of the TM program on productivity in 1972. Frew had been concerned with the negative effects of stress on performance and was impressed with early data suggesting the TM technique as a natural and powerful tool for reducing accumulated stress and improving ability to handle pressure.

Though the TM program apparently produced changes which would contribute to improved performance, the question remained whether improvement in performance would show up on the job.

Might the increased energy and well-being derived from the TM program be directed toward personal rather than professional pursuits? Would the reduction in stress and increase in self-acceptance and psychological well-being somehow inhibit motivation? Could increased creativity among meditators increase *dis*satisfaction with repetitive jobs and therefore increase turnover? If the Transcendental Meditation program does improve job performance, would executives and rank-and-file employees show improvement of similar magnitude?

To answer these questions, Frew conducted two studies. The first was completed in 1973 and published in the *Academy of Management Journal*.[1] The second study was completed in early 1975 and presented at the American Management Associations' Annual Personnel Conference.[2] "Taken together," wrote Frew, "I feel that the two studies systematically provide thorough scientific evidence for the powerful impact of the Transcendental Meditation program on productivity."[3]

The First Study: Design

Frew's first study aimed at determining the impact of the TM program on six measures of productivity among a group of 100 people working full time. His study population included 68 men and 32 women who had practiced the TM program for an average of 13 months. The group included both executives and rank-and-file employees from a number of different firms. Each participant completed a questionnaire about changes at work since starting the TM program. The questionnaire produced data concerning the following six factors:

Job satisfaction
Performance
Turnover potential
Relationship with supervisor
Relationship with others
Motivation to climb

The study included two controls. First, nonmeditating supervisors or co-workers of the meditators evaluated changes in how the meditators performed before and after learning the TM technique. The supervisors and co-workers completed a questionnaire similar to that which the meditators filled out. The supervisors' questionnaire was simply reworded to refer to a third person rather than to the person completing it. The second control consisted of graduate students who were working full time and who had undertaken any program or had any experience which they felt had "improved their lives" in the recent past. The particular experiences reported by the graduate students varied from "management seminars" to "peak experiences." The graduate students completed a questionnaire identical to that of the meditators, but filled it out in terms of their own non-TM experiences.

The First Study: Results, Discussion, Criticisms

The results of the study are presented in Figure 5(a). The meditators reported significant improvement in job satisfaction and job performance. They also reported significantly improved relations with supervisors and co-workers. Finally, the meditators' propensity to change jobs and their climb orientation decreased significantly.

Results from the controls confirmed all but one of these findings. First, the graduate students showed no significant changes in any of the factors measured. Second, the co-workers and supervisors agreed that, since starting the TM program, the meditators seemed more satisfied at work, showed greater output and efficiency, got along better with supervisors and co-workers, and seemed less likely to leave the company. The supervisors disagreed on the estimate of climb orientation. While the meditators felt *less* concerned about promotions, supervisors observed that the meditators seemed to have *increased* in climb-oriented behavior.

Frew suggests that the data from the first study constitute solid evidence that the TM program improves productivity. Concerning the disagreement among meditators and nonmeditating supervisors about TM's impact on climb orientation, Frew argues that the TM program may increase behavior leading to promotion, but decreases anxiety about it. In today's work environment, where promotion-anxiety contributes to much wasted energy in politicking and back-stabbing, the reduction in promotion-anxiety may not be the least important effect of the TM program.

Frew further analyzed his data by comparing the changes reported by the meditating executives with those of nonmanagerial meditators. He found that executives showed significantly greater productivity increases after starting the TM program than did hourly employees. These data are summarized in Figure 5(b). Frew also found that meditators working in democratic organiza-

Figure 5. Increased productivity.

(a)

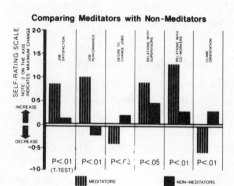

(b)

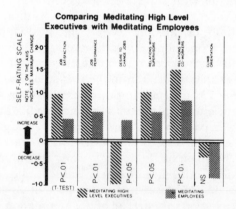

Source: *Fundamentals of Progress*, MIU Press Publication No. U2-16-575, © 1975 Maharishi International University. Research results were originally reported in D. R. Frew, "Transcendental Meditation and Productivity," *Academy of Management Journal*, Vol. 17, No. 2., pp. 362–368, June 1974.

tions showed greater productivity increases than those working in more autocratically managed work environments.

Frew reports that three consistent criticisms of his first study prompted him to undertake a second. These criticisms were that the first study was too small, that it did not adequately compare meditators with nonmeditators, and that the questionnaire may have lacked validity. To answer these criticisms, Frew modified the design of his second study in the following ways: First, he expanded the size of his second study to include 250 meditators and 250 nonmeditators. Second, he distributed the same questionnaire to each of the 500 subjects participating in the study and focused his statistical analysis of results on comparing the meditators with the nonmeditators. Finally, he designed an entirely new questionnaire. He hypothesized that if a completely different kind of questionnaire produced the same results as were produced by the first study, then the validity of both questionnaires would certainly be strengthened.

The Second Study: Design, Results, Conclusions

To randomize selection of subjects as much as possible, Frew enlisted the 500 subjects in the second study from more than 30 states and two provinces in Canada. Subjects for the first study lived fairly close to Erie, Pennsylvania. Of the 250 control subjects, 125 were graduate students in an M.B.A. program but were holding down full-time jobs. In redesigning the questionnaire for the second study, Frew added questions which would measure three additional factors of productivity:

1. Job content satisfaction (how much an employee enjoys the specific content of his work rather than his work in general).
2. Perceived image (to what extent an employee feels his colleagues at work view him as competent and useful).
3. Organizational satisfaction (how the employee feels about the organization as a whole).

The results of the second study demonstrated even more clearly than the first that the TM program improved productivity. Whereas statistical analysis suggested that results of the first study deserved 95 percent confidence, statistical analysis revealed that the data compiled in the second study deserved 99.9 percent confidence (p < .001).* On the basis of his two studies, Frew noted that in comparison with nonmeditators, people practicing the TM program:

Experience a higher level of job satisfaction.
Are more productive in terms of output criteria.
Are less apt to want to leave their companies.
Enjoy better relationships with their supervisors.
Have better interpersonal relationships with their co-workers.
Have a lower anxiety about climbing the organizational ladder.
Enjoy their individual work assignments to a larger extent.
Have a better perception of their external image.
Appear to be more highly satisfied with their own organizations.[4]

Close examination of the second study data suggests additional conclusions about how the TM program affects productivity. First, the 250 nonmeditators reported significant dissatisfaction with the content of their jobs and with the organizations in which they worked. The nonmeditators expressed what many behavioral scientists have identified as a sweeping complaint against work in America. In this light, it is particularly interesting to note that 13 months of the TM program fosters sufficient individual growth to increase both job content satisfaction and regard for the organization. Frew also analyzed his second study data by length of time practicing the technique of TM. He found that people practicing the TM program for more than one year showed significantly greater productivity gains than those people practicing it less than one year. Statistical analysis suggests 99 percent confidence in this result.

One further aspect of the study deserves mention: Graduate students generally show higher productivity than the average worker. By including 125 graduate students in his control group, Frew biased the control group toward showing increased productivity. He therefore lessened the differences in observed productivity gains which might be expected in a comparison of a random group of people practicing TM with a truly random group of workers not practicing TM. That a random 250 people practicing TM showed significantly greater productivity than a group of 250 people generally above average in productivity strengthens Frew's findings.

*In most scientific research, 95 percent confidence is the minimal basis acceptable for drawing conclusions from a set of results.

The TM Program in Companies

Initial reports from a variety of companies offering in-house Transcendental Meditation programs to executives and/or other employees support Frew's findings. No company has yet completed a large-scale in-house study of how the TM program affects the company's long-term performance. Nevertheless, a growing number of firms from many different industries are reporting that the TM program is a valuable addition to their organizational development program. Firms exploring TM range in size and industry from small privately owned firms to the largest corporations in the world.

Since 1973, E. R. Polk, chairman of P.A. Medical Corporation, has been encouraging management and labor in two plants to begin the Transcendental Meditation program. In one of the plants, 50 percent of the administrative staff practice TM. As a result, Polk reports:

> We have found that the executives and the employees are working together more effectively and accomplishing greater productivity. Absenteeism has decreased significantly. The general atmosphere of the plant has markedly improved, and the working conditions seem to be more pleasant and acceptable.[5]

Blue Cross–Blue Shield in Chicago has been experimenting with the TM program since mid-1975. Interest among top management prompted the training director to set up an in-house TM program for 30 managers. The group was so impressed with the program after six months that the company has decided to set up a second course open to all executives and employees.

Gil Younger is president of Transco, a small manufacturer of transmission parts in southern California. He began introducing the TM program to his firm in 1972 when he learned the technique. Transco has grown spectacularly over the past four years despite the recession. Younger reports that productivity and sales dollars per employee have almost doubled. Because the firm is small, Younger has introduced no development programs other than TM. Furthermore, he can find no specific reason, in new manufacturing or marketing techniques, for the dramatic growth of Transco.

Lauretta Cessario, personnel officer at Upper Avenue National Bank in Chicago, reports favorable results with an in-house TM program. Approximately 10 percent of the management staff participated in the bank's first TM course. Improved human relations were, according to Ms. Cessario, the most noticeable results of the program. The second in-house TM course will double the percentage of the management staff practicing the TM program.

Several branches of the armed services are teaching the TM program to their personnel. Major General Franklin Davis, recently retired commandant of the U.S. Army War College, is largely responsible for initial interest in the TM program among the services. Assigned by the Joint Chiefs of Staff to determine how to reduce drug abuse in the armed services, Major General Davis discovered that the TM program does much more than reduce drug abuse. Courses in the TM program are now given regularly at West Point Military Academy and army bases throughout the world. The U.S. Air Force now makes air-base facilities available for military personnel to take the TM program.

Summary

People practicing the TM program appear to become more productive and more satisfied with their work within a relatively short time after starting the program. Regular practice of the technique seems to contribute to steady, cumulative improvement in performance, human relations, job satisfaction, and regard for the organization.

It appears that the increased personal satisfaction resulting from the TM program provides an experiential base for increased satisfaction at work. Fears that increased psychological well-being might decrease motivation, that increased creativity would exacerbate job dissatisfaction, or that increased energy would find personal rather than professional outlets seem to be unfounded. Though people practicing the Transcendental Meditation technique may lose their anxiety about promotion, they show improved regard for the organization and increased likelihood of promotion due to improved performance. Whether people practicing the TM technique outgrow their jobs more rapidly than non-meditators remains to be determined.

Finally, subjective reports do indicate that people practicing TM enjoy their personal lives much more after starting the program. They have more time, energy, creativity, and love for their families and friends. Nevertheless, a substantial portion of the increased energy, intelligence, and creativity resulting from the TM program gets channeled into professional pursuits.

NOTES

1. D. R. Frew, "Transcendental Meditation and Productivity." *Academy of Management Journal*, Vol. 17, No. 2, June 1974.
2. "AMA Annual Personnel Conference," *BNA Bulletin to Management*, No. 1309, March 13, 1975.
3. D. R. Frew, *The Management of Stress: Using Meditation at Work*. Chicago: Nelson Hall, in press.
4. Ibid.
5. Personal correspondence.

5
Looking Ahead: TM and the Horizons of Progress

Subjective reports and objective research indicate that the TM program boosts performance at work and enhances life at home. This growth adds up to improved self-regard, increased satisfaction with the job, and more loyalty to the organization. In the final section of this account, I want to consider a potpourri of important issues concerning the TM program. What implications does the TM program have for management theory in general? What are the most often expressed criticisms of the TM program? What can the TM program contribute to the future of management?

The TM program represents a new and unique approach to developing the human resources of organizations. It is a simple program which fosters growth through natural physiological changes. It is easy and does not require group process. Most managers hold to the unquestioned belief, however, that unlocking human potential is a difficult, complex, and unpredictable affair. The continuing debate over whether organization development really works fuels this belief. The idea that personal success requires struggle, even at the expense of a rich family life, further contributes to this conviction. How could an effortless technique, which does not require any interpersonal confrontation, improve people's performance in business? Isn't the idea that growth is easy through the TM program at odds with the most basic work ethic of business?

These questions almost inevitably trouble a manager when he or she first learns about TM. Even when they are not expressed they often fester beneath the surface of nonspecific fears or doubts. In fact, the TM program does challenge the belief that accelerating human development is difficult, complex, and unpredictable. Because the TM program takes advantage of natural physiological processes and depends for its effectiveness on laws of nature, it is easy, simple, and systematic. The TM program challenges the Protestant work ethic in the same way that the power shovel challenges the belief that digging a 60-foot trench must be a drudgery.

Hard work has certainly been and continues to be an important element in the success of business. Of even greater importance to continued progress in business, however, is a basic principle of technological advancement: *By taking advantage of natural laws, a person can do less and accomplish more.* The impossible becomes possible. The TM program may constitute a discovery in the technology of human development equal in importance to the great achievements in industrial technology. Just as technological achievements in industry have changed management theory, the TM program also suggests a corresponding advance in the theory of management.

The Absolute Theory of Management

The old saying that "most problems are self-created" applies to organizations as well as individuals. Different systems of management may be appropriate for different industries and different-size organizations. The problems in most organizations arise not because the management system is inadequate, but because people in the organization make mistakes. The absolute theory of management formulated by Maharishi Mahesh Yogi aims at eliminating mistakes by expanding the consciousness of the people working in the organization. Every person in an organization, from the assembly-line worker to the president, must manage his sphere of responsibility. Mistakes at any level of the organization are costly. The absolute theory of management identifies those qualities necessary for the manager to avoid mistakes.

The absolute theory of management has its foundation in natural law. Nature is a remarkable manager. Only cursory examination of even the simplest living organism is sufficient to demonstrate the superb managerial capabilities of all living things. Three basic qualities appear to be essential to the management of natural processes. The absolute theory suggests that if people in an organization possessed these qualities, they would automatically enlist the support of all the laws of nature in their every action. They would manage their activity in accordance with nature and thereby avoid mistakes.

The first quality essential to management in nature is order. The manager must be more orderly than what he manages, because management is a process of giving direction and creating order. The DNA molecule is an exquisite example of order as the basis for management of natural processes. DNA is so highly ordered that it can give chemical instructions which sustain the life of a cell under a wide range of environmental circumstances. The quantum field is another excellent example of order at the basis of nature. Quantum field theory postulates a field of zero entropy as a state of maximum order underlying all sub-atomic particles. Minute fluctuations in this field are said to create, maintain, and destroy matter, but the field itself always remains at zero entropy.

The second quality fundamental to nature's managerial method is minimal excitation. Natural systems give new directions to matter and energy with the least possible effort and excitation. To take another biological example, the enzyme perfectly illustrates this principle. Enzymes reduce the amount of energy necessary for chemical reactions to take place. Chemical reactions which would happen very infrequently under normal conditions will occur very rapidly in the presence of an enzyme. In facilitating a chemical reaction, however, the enzyme does not *do* anything. It expends no energy and does not change chemically. The enzyme manages its task simply by coming in close contact with the compounds which require catalysis to react.

The third quality essential to nature's managerial skill is openness to all possibilities. Nature structures growth to increase the choices available to organisms. Rising on the evolutionary ladder from one-celled organisms to man, the importance of instinct decreases and the ability to adapt increases. Growth apparently requires an openness to an ever wider horizon of possibilities.

How important to effective organizational management are orderliness, minimum excitation, and maximum openness to possibilities? These qualities constitute the foundation of management itself. No matter where a person works in an organization, his action depends on the quality of his thinking. A disorderly mind is fertile ground for mistakes in even the simplest of activities. If a programmer comes to work with a cloudy mind, the frequency of computer errors and improperly conveyed messages increases sharply. By contrast, an orderly mind is the prerequisite of creative problem solving. Only an orderly mind can keep track of all the elements of a problem simultaneously and come up with a solution which takes all the elements into account.

Minimum excitation is equally important to effective action. Managers value "calm under pressure," because this calm permits a person to remain clear-headed in the face of pressure to find a solution to the problem at hand. This clear-headed and calm state is consonant with minimal internal excitation. When a person's mind is agitated, he tends to make hasty decisions. A high level of internal excitation is also a fertile ground for mistakes. Minimal excitation of the mind is as important to clear thinking as minimal "noise" is to a clear electrical signal. Physics defines an inverse relation between order and excitation. Minimal excitation generally accompanies maximum order.

Possibility is a key word for management. The more possibilities a manager can realize in an orderly fashion, the greater are his chances for optimizing the functioning of the system he manages. Whether a difficult situation becomes an obstacle or an opportunity depends upon the manager's vision. If a manager has a limited vision about how he should handle his responsibilities, he will meet many more obstacles than opportunities. If, on the other hand, a manager can freely entertain a wide range of possibilities in any given situation, he will regularly turn obstacles into opportunities.

An orderly mind which maintains a state of least excitation and maximum openness is the basis of management. When a person develops these qualities, he enlists the support of nature in his efforts to manage his activity, because these qualities are fundamental to how nature manages. He avoids mistakes and maximizes growth. The absolute theory of management suggests that developing these qualities within a significant number of people working in any organization will substantially reduce the problems of that organization. Through the physiological changes resulting from the TM program, the individual establishes his consciousness in the field of greatest order, least excitation, and maximum openness to all possibilities.

Criticisms

Four criticisms of the TM program most often concern people in business. The first and most widely expressed is that even though TM is easy, systematic, and practical, the name conjures up visions of mysticism and a general withdrawal from practical life. This misunderstanding disappears after the first 10 minutes spent in learning what the TM program involves. Nevertheless, many people in business quietly ask themselves, "What will my boss think if he hears that I practice the TM program?"

As long as people confuse the TM program with other techniques which go by the name of meditation or yoga, this criticism will have some validity. People in business must be concerned lest they develop an image of being impractical or wasting time. The educational organization which teaches the TM program is taking several steps to overcome this confusion in the public mind. First, the TM program is service marked. Second, a public information campaign involving appearances on national television talk shows, articles in the national press, and publication of several new books on the TM program (one of which was a recent best·seller) is increasing public knowledge about TM. Third, symposiums and seminars on the TM program are offered regularly around the country to inform the business community about the TM program. With nearly a million Americans now practicing the TM program—including senators, astronauts, presidents of some of America's largest corporations, and famous athletes—the association with mysticism is rapidly disappearing.

A second criticism of the TM program is that it takes too much time. To gain significant benefits from the program, the technique *must* be practiced twice a day for 20 minutes. Many busy executives ask themselves how they will ever find 20 minutes twice a day to practice the TM technique, but this concern arises in the minds of people unfamiliar with the program. Once a person begins practicing the technique regularly, the time requirements cease to be a problem. One chief executive of a very large pharmaceuticals company criticized the TM organizations for not making it clear enough that 40 minutes of TM daily actually *saves* time. He told me emphatically: "You should say, 'Net, it saves time. You're more relaxed. You sleep better. You get things done more quickly and easily. So, you *save* time.' It's a little sales pitch—but it's *true*." Another executive noted: "It's not like an exercise program or a diet. TM is enjoyable, so you look forward to doing it twice a day."

The third major criticism of the TM program is directed against its uniqueness. People often ask whether they cannot get the same results from a relaxation exercise or a nap. NTL and other management development organizations teach relaxation exercises. From a superficial standpoint, the TM technique may appear to be simply a relaxation exercise. But as we have seen, physiological studies of the brain's electrical activity show that this technique produces more than relaxation. The most significant physiological change during the practice of the TM technique is not bodily relaxation but coherent brain waves. Thus the TM program really is unique.

The fourth major criticism concerns implementation of in-house courses. If top management introduces a TM program, won't employees feel coerced into taking the course? This problem has been overcome in some companies by democratizing the decision to introduce a TM program. Instead of top management simply announcing a TM program by fiat, people from various levels of the organization recommend adoption or rejection of the program after hearing an introductory presentation about the technique and its benefits.

Criticisms of the TM program arise primarily from ignorance about what the program actually involves. No negative effects of the Transcendental Meditation technique have been reported in the numerous scientific publications on the effects of the program, and serious criticism of the program itself is very hard to find. In general, even people who once learned the TM technique and fail to practice it regularly speak positively about its effects. As one chief executive put it, "How can people object to the fact that they may be more efficient, more relaxed, more alert, and more energetic?"

Transcendental Meditation and the Future of Business

Productivity, job satisfaction, and employee health are perhaps the three most important personnel issues facing business over the next decade. Legislation to safeguard employee health and group approaches to increase productivity or job satisfaction are falling far short of achieving the improvements necessary to guarantee the continued success of American business. The TM program appears capable of making a significant contribution in all three of these areas. The significance of the TM program for business was anticipated as early as 1972 by Francis Barret, president of Management Concepts Ltd., in Canada. In an interview, Barret predicted that "within ten years the Transcendental Meditation program will be taught in over 50 percent of North American executive training programs."

Constantine Anagnostopoulos, general manager of Monsanto's New Enterprise Division, suggested that the TM program may open a new dimension in the effort to increase productivity. "The extension of the American executive up to now has been primarily mechanical—for example, through the computer," he said. "Transcendental Meditation extends the physiological and psychological capabilities of the person. If an executive can work a full eight hours at peak mental clarity, rather than five or six, he's obviously going to be more productive. It's a new dimension." Hartzel Lebed, senior vice-president of Connecticut General Corporation, suggested that "Business can use every source of help possible in increasing productivity and creativity. The Transcendental Meditation program is very useful in this regard. It wouldn't surprise me if business showed steadily increasing interest in the Transcendental Meditation program to increase productivity."

Few personnel problems are as knotty as that of job satisfaction. A variety of organization development techniques based on several different theories of human nature have produced only marginal results in improving job satisfaction. But we don't need theories about human nature to understand how the TM program can improve job satisfaction. The relation between physiological well-being and the enjoyment of life is quite simple: When a person feels lousy, he tends to transfer his feeling to his work. When he feels good, he will transfer good feelings to his work. By reducing stress and increasing integration of physiological functions, the TM program fosters the natural experience of well-being. Alexander Poniotoff, founder and chairman emeritus of Ampex Corporation, wrote: "Even after a few months of practicing, I am convinced that TM could not only efficiently solve the problem of tension and stress, and, as a result, improve health, but could also contribute substantially to helping people find greater satisfaction in their work."

Health is a growing concern in business for a variety of reasons. The federal government has passed legislation mandating improved health and safety conditions in business. The cost of losing a top executive to coronary disease is considerable. The general public is becoming increasingly health conscious. Research indicates that the TM program reduces high blood pressure, stress, anxiety, insomnia, and use of alcohol and cigarettes, the five factors that constitute today's most serious threats to health. Additional research indicates that the TM program alleviates psychosomatic disorders and improves resistance to disease. The TM program may also improve safety by increasing alertness, reaction time, and perceptual-motor performance. For these reasons, Harold H. Bloomfield, M.D., author of the best-selling book *TM: Discovering Inner Energy and Overcoming Stress*, wrote that "Transcendental Meditation is a physiological necessity in our modern world of stress and strain." In an interview, David Doner, M.D., chief of the Renal Division at the Boston VA Hospital, has said: "TM must be counted among the high technologies of medicine, such as vaccines, because TM prevents disease. TM is the healthiest thing I do."

Conclusion

In the coming decades, unfolding human potential may prove more important to the continued vitality of American business than technological achievements. The dissatisfaction people feel toward their jobs undermines their commitment to work and must be overcome if progress in business is to continue. The TM program appears to be a unique and highly effective approach to unfolding full individual potential and increasing personal well-being at work and at home.

An individual need not depend on others to grow through the TM program. Because the TM program does not involve group process, the program is much simpler, much less time-consuming, and much less apt to meet resistance than most other organization development techniques.

American business thrives on healthy competition because it inspires people to draw on their inner resources and perform at their best. The competitive spirit weaves teamwork out of individual strength. If the people who make up a team are weak, the competitive spirit falters in inefficiency, poor interpersonal relations, and failure. The TM program revitalizes a healthy competitive spirit by directly strengthening the individual.

TM's uniqueness lies in its ability to foster comprehensive, balanced growth. Unlike approaches which develop specific skills or qualities, the TM program enriches every aspect of a person's life simultaneously by expanding consciousness through physiological integration. The TM program apparently brings the individual to a state of awareness that enables him to draw on great reserves of energy, intelligence, and creativity at the deepest levels of the mind. By establishing individual awareness in a state of maximum order, least excitation, and maximum receptiveness, the TM program may prove capable of greatly reducing individual error and thereby reducing problems in any system of management.

The TM program is not a fad. "The Transcendental Meditation program," said the president of one of America's largest companies, "is the simplest, most direct, and most effective means of developing people I've seen. It achieves in people what all those behavioral science fellows have been talking about. It works, and it's here to stay."

Appendix A

THE TECHNIQUE OF TRANSCENDENTAL MEDITATION:
Questions and Answers

The technique of TM is unique, in that it cannot be learned from a book or a do-it-yourself cassette. To learn the TM technique properly, a person must receive instruction from a qualified teacher of the TM program. Qualified teachers are active in 400 centers throughout the United States and in 61 countries around the world. In this appendix, I have tried to answer briefly some of the most frequently asked questions about the TM technique.

What happens when you learn the TM technique?

The Transcendental Meditation technique is effortless and natural. It involves simply allowing the mind to experience increasingly subtle impulses of thought, finally transcending the conscious thinking process altogether, and to experience the source of thought. To facilitate this process, a person uses a *particular* thought as a vehicle for the mind to experience increasingly quiet impulses of thought. The sanskrit word for the thought-vehicles used during TM is *mantra*, which means a sound whose effects are completely known. The principle effect of a mantra used properly during the TM technique is to soothe body and mind.

When a person learns the Transcendental Meditation technique, he learns two things: First, his instructor gives him an appropriate mantra. Dr. Bernard Glueck noted: "Maharishi insists that the mantra is the critical factor in the technique. On the basis of our research, we tend to agree with this." Second, and equally important, the person's instructor shows him how to use the mantra properly. Mantras used during the practice of the TM technique have no linguistic meaning. Consequently, the technique does not involve contemplation or thinking about things. Also, the mantra used properly in TM is not a point of focus or concentration. Neither a process of contemplation nor concentration, the technique of TM allows the mind to entertain increasingly vague and refined impulses of the mantra until the mind transcends the mantra and settles into a state of pure consciousness.

When learned properly, this process is entirely effortless, because the correct practice of the TM technique makes use of the natural tendency of the mind to move toward increasing happiness. As you read this page, you may be fully absorbed in it. If your favorite piece of music were to come on the radio, however, your mind might *automatically* shift from reading to listening. The innate desire to experience increasing happiness is the impelling force behind this automatic shift of attention. During instruction in the TM program, a person learns how to make use of this natural tendency of the mind to meditate properly. He finds that the mind will automatically settle down to increasingly refined experiences of the mantra because each step of this process brings a feeling of increasing well-being.

Is silence, a special posture, or any particular environment necessary for Transcendental Meditation?

No. The TM technique can be practiced anywhere. Executives sometimes practice TM while riding in airplanes, commuter trains, or cars. TM can even be practiced on buses and the subway. All that is necessary to practice TM is a reasonably comfortable chair and an opportunity to close the eyes for 20 minutes. A person practicing TM appears to be simply relaxing with the eyes closed or perhaps sleeping. Noise is absolutely no barrier to the correct practice of TM, and no special posture is required other than sitting comfortably.

Why do TM for just 20 minutes twice a day, and not more or less?

TM is a preparation for activity. A person does not practice TM for the experience of the meditation, but for beneficial effects following the brief meditation period. Twenty minutes of TM has proven sufficient to sustain energy, mental clarity, and emotional ease for about eight hours. To live the fullest possible day, a person does 20 minutes of TM before breakfast to sustain peak performance at work and another 20 minutes at the end of the working day to recharge and enjoy evening activity.

Must TM be practiced at the same time every day?

No. The rule of thumb for judging when to meditate is: Meditate after you get up in the morning and again six to eight hours later. TM is not recommended immediately after meals, because the physiology of digestion inhibits the physiology of TM. TM is also not recommended before going to sleep, because TM increases wakefulness.

Does anyone fail to learn TM?

No. The Transcendental Meditation technique is simple and natural; anyone can learn it properly. Teachers of the Transcendental Meditation program are highly trained and capable of teaching anyone to practice properly.

Who teaches the technique?

The World Plan Executive Council is a nonprofit educational organization established in more than 60 countries around the world to teach the Transcendental Meditation program. This parent organization has several educational service divisions, each of which offers TM courses to different segments of society. In the United States the American Foundation for the Science of Creative Intelligence (AFSCI) teaches courses to business and government.

These divisions have officers, staff, and line personnel at the international, national, and local levels. Nearly all the employees of the organization have completed all training necessary to become a qualified instructor of the TM program. This teacher-training course is offered in a variety of residential and nonresidential formats by the World Plan Executive Council.

The principal teaching facility for the Transcendental Meditation program is the local World Plan Center. Each of the five divisions of the U.S. World Plan Executive Council operates through the 400 World Plan Centers throughout the United States. The U.S. organization is affiliated with an accredited college, Maharishi International University, which has a 2,000-room campus in Fairfield, Iowa, where MIU makes its U.S. headquarters. The World Plan Executive Council in the United States also owns several large residential facilities for advanced courses given in residence.

Where does TM come from?

The teaching of transcending as the way to develop full human potential first appears in the oldest written record of human experience, the *Vedas*. Passed on for thousands of years, the TM technique has not been widely practiced correctly, even in India, for many generations. Revived in the twentieth century by a great Indian sage, Transcendental Meditation was brought to the Western world by his student, Maharishi Mahesh Yogi.

The present revival of TM is overcoming the long-misguided beliefs that meditation is difficult, produces results only after many years, requires special diets and postures, and demands withdrawal from life. All these ideas have arisen in the absence of knowledge about how to practice the Transcendental Meditation technique correctly. In cooperation with scientists all over the world, Maharishi has founded a new academic discipline, the Science of Creative Intelligence, based on the unfoldment of full human potential through TM. This science studies the origin, range, and development of creative intelligence, and opens the possibility of full human development to scientific inquiry. Through this inquiry, the superstitions about Transcendental Meditation are being dispelled. Scientific knowledge about how Transcendental Meditation releases human potential is leading to the application of Transcendental Meditation programs to all areas of society.

Is TM a religion, or does it interfere with religion?

No. People of all faiths practice TM. Priests, nuns, rabbis, ministers, and atheists all practice TM and endorse the technique for its contribution to human well-being. TM does not require adherence to any set of beliefs or any particular philosophy. TM is simply a technique which produces a variety of beneficial effects which may be studied scientifically.

Is Transcendental Meditation like hypnosis, or does it involve hypnosis?

No. The technique of TM produces the state of restful alertness which is distinctly different from a trance state. During TM, a person is necessarily very relaxed; during hypnosis, relaxation may or may not be present. During TM, a person is least subject to the power of suggestion; during hypnosis, a person is most subject to suggestion. During TM, mind-body coordination is increased; during hypnosis, mind-body coordination may be diminished (i.e., a person can eat an onion and taste an orange). Physiological studies show that during TM oxygen consumption drops 16 to 20 percent and brain waves become highly orderly; no such changes have been found during hypnosis.

Do some people stop meditating after they learn the technique? If so, why?

Dr. Shaffi, a psychiatrist at the University of Michigan, found that 70 percent of the people who learn TM continue to practice the technique regularly. In general, even people who practice it irregularly speak highly of the technique. The principal reason why people become irregular is failure to follow the program as instructed.

It is recommended that a person who has learned TM have the correct practice of the technique verified. This verification procedure, called "checking," is best done several times within the first month and monthly for the first year after learning the technique. "Checking" takes about 20 minutes and is available at all TM centers. If a person does not follow this regimen, he may begin to meditate incorrectly, experience a gradual diminution of results, and become irregular in his practice.

How long does a person have to meditate in order to get results?

The Transcendental Meditation program produces both immediate and cumulative results, including all the physiological changes which accompany the correct practice of the technique.

With regular practice of the TM technique for 20 minutes twice daily, people begin to experience improvements in mental functioning, general health, interpersonal relationships, and performance. Many people notice these benefits in their daily activity within the first several weeks, some notice benefits within the first few days, and others may not notice significant benefits for several months.

Because the TM technique produces results through physiological changes, correct practice of the technique guarantees that anyone will eventually notice significant benefits in their lives, even though they may not even be aware of the changes taking place. This may be because the technique produces balanced and natural growth, which is not always noticeable from day to day. Who notices that a child has grown from one day to the next? Over a six-month period, however, a child's growth is very obvious.

If a person experiences the immediate results of TM, then he is practicing the technique properly and can be certain that the cumulative benefits are accruing in his life with each meditation. "It's not each meditation," said one executive, "but it's two meditations a day for a week, a month, several months, or a year that produces really fantastic benefits, and the benefits just keep growing."

How does TM compare with other meditation techniques?

Meditation techniques other than TM fall into two categories: concentration and contemplation. Comtemplative techniques are those which involve thinking about things—brotherhood, love, God, and so on. Concentrative techniques are those which involve controlling the mind. The technique of TM involves neither concentration nor contemplation and is a wholly natural process.

Unlike some other systems, the TM program is taught systematically all over the world. In addition, where some other techniques are very difficult, require changes in belief or lifestyle, and produce results only after many years of practice, the TM program is easy, requires no changes in belief or lifestyle, and produces both immediate and cumulative results. It represents a return to the understanding of what meditation is and how to practice it properly.

How do you begin the Transcendental Meditation program?

The TM program is available through centers for Transcendental Meditation all over the world. The core of the program is a seven-step procedure during which a person learns the Transcendental Meditation technique. These steps are:

	Topic	Time
1. Introductory lecture	What is TM?	1½ hours
2. Preparatory lecture	How does TM work?	1½ hours
3. Personal interview with TM instructor		5 to 10 minutes
4. Personal instruction		2 hours
5. Verification and validation of correct practice; group instruction	Correct and incorrect practice	2 hours
6. Verification and validation of correct practice; group instruction	The mechanics of the Transcendental Meditation technique	2 hours
7. Verification and validation of correct practice; group and private instruction	The evolution of consciousness through the TM program	2 hours

Steps 4–7 must be completed on four consecutive days.

In order to assure correct practice and maximum benefit, three additional elements of the Transcendental Meditation program are available: checking, advanced lectures, and residence courses. Checking is a procedure of verifying that a person is practicing the TM technique correctly. Advanced lectures offer further intellectual understanding about growth through the TM program. They also provide insight into the Science of Creative Intelligence, a new science of which the TM program is the practical aspect. Residence courses consist of a two- or three-day program of profound rest through TM and intellectual growth through study of the Science of Creative Intelligence. These courses provide an invaluable opportunity for a giant step in personal growth.

When TM programs are offered on an in-house basis, AFSCI designs the program to suit the company's size, needs, and ongoing training activities for management and labor.

Appendix B

SELECTED SCIENTIFIC EVIDENCE
ON THE BENEFITS OF TM

The charts and discussions in this appendix are reprinted from
Scientific Research on the Transcendental Meditation Programme,
MIU Press Publication No. G205, © Maharishi International University. Rheinweiler, West Germany, 1975.

CHART 1
Normalization of High Blood Pressure

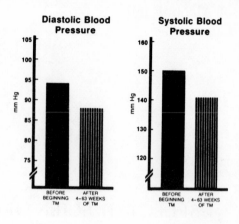

Diastolic Blood Pressure

mm Hg

105
100
95
90
85
80
75

BEFORE BEGINNING TM — AFTER 4–63 WEEKS OF TM

Systolic Blood Pressure

mm Hg

160
150
140
130
120

BEFORE BEGINNING TM — AFTER 4–63 WEEKS OF TM

Finding: Systolic and diastolic arterial blood pressure was recorded 1,119 times in 22 hypertensive patients before and after they began the Transcendental Meditation program. The decreases in blood pressure after patients began practicing Transcendental Meditation were statistically significant. These findings indicate that the Transcendental Meditation program is useful and effective as an adjunct in the treatment of high blood pressure.

Interpretation: In the United States alone essential hypertension affects over 23 million citizens, including one out of every three adult males. High blood pressure increases the risk of death and disease due to heart attack, stroke, and damage to vital organs. Autonomic lability (instability) has been shown to be a precursor to hypertension. The Transcendental Meditation program promotes autonomic stability and may be important in both the treatment of hypertension and the prevention of cardiovascular disease.

First reference: Herbert Benson and Robert Keith Wallace, "Decreased Blood Pressure in Hypertensive Subjects Who Practiced Meditation," Supplement II to *Circulation* 45 and 46 (1972). Reprinted in *Scientific Research on the Transcendental Meditation Program: Collected Papers*, vol. 1, ed. David W. Orme-Johnson and John T. Farrow (New York: MIU Press, 1975).

Second reference: Barry Blackwell, Irwin Hanenson, Saul Bloomfield, Herbert Magenheim, Sanford Nidich, and Peter Gartside, "Effects of Transcendental Meditation on Blood Pressure: A Controlled Pilot Experiment," *Journal of Psychosomatic Medicine* (in press). Reprinted in *Scientific Research on the Transcendental Meditation Program: Collected Papers*, vol. 1, ed. David W. Orme-Johnson and John T. Farrow (New York: MIU Press, 1975).

CHART 2
Reduced Use of Alcohol and Cigarettes

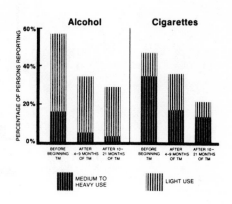

Finding: A retrospective study of 1,862 subjects who had practiced the Transcendental Meditation technique a mean of 20 months showed a significant reduction in the reported use of alcohol and cigarettes.

Interpretation: In other research, Transcendental Meditation has been shown to provide deep relaxation to the entire nervous system and to remove tensions, giving rise to a more calm, restful, and creative functioning of mind and body. These effects may be taken to explain the gradual decrease in the need for alcohol and cigarettes seen in this study.

Reference: Herbert Benson and Robert Keith Wallace, "Decreased Drug Abuse with Transcendental Meditation: A Study of 1,862 Subjects," *Drug Abuse: Proceedings of the International Conference*, ed. Chris J. D. Zarafonetis (Philadelphia: Lea and Febiger, 1972): 369–376 and *Congressional Record*, Serial No. 92–1 (Washington, D.C.; U.S. Government Printing Office, 1971). Reprinted in *Scientific Research on the Transcendental Meditation Program: Collected Papers*, vol. 1, ed. David W. Orme-Johnson and John T. Farrow (New York: MIU Press, 1975).

CHART 3
Improved Resistance to Disease

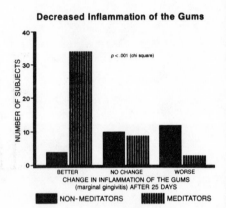

Decreased Inflammation of the Gums

Finding: Forty-six persons practicing the Transcendental Meditation technique were clinically examined for a common inflammation of the gums before and after a special course involving extended meditation. The improvement in the individuals practicing the Transcendental Meditation Technique was marked and significantly greater than in control subjects.

Interpretation: Health of the gums is considered to be a good reflection of overall health. Furthermore, gum inflammation is known to have a high correlation with level of stress. This study indicates that the Transcendental Meditation program increases resistance to disease and strengthens the immune system generally, a profound biochemical effect that comes about on the basis of a more relaxed style of functioning of mind and body.

Reference: Ira M. Klemons, "Change in Inflammation in Persons Practicing the Transcendental Meditation Technique" (Pennsylvania State University, University Park, Pennsylvania), *Scientific Research on the Transcendental Meditation Program: Collected Papers*, vol. 1, ed. David W. Orme-Johnson and John T. Farrow (New York: MIU Press, 1975).

CHART 4
Relief
from Insomnia

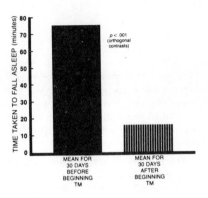

Finding: Transcendental Meditation significantly reduced the time taken for insomniacs to fall asleep. As a therapy against insomnia, the Transcendental Meditation program was reported to be (1) simple to administer, (2) immediately effective, (3) stable over time, and (4) without unfavorable side effects.

Interpretation: The Transcendental Meditation technique relieves deep-seated stress from the nervous system on a direct physiological level. Consequently, it produces a wide range of beneficial effects without requiring specific attention to any one area. The effect seen here, greater regularity in the sleeping cycle, reflects a stabilization of basic biological rhythms, one aspect of a holistic stabilization of daily life.

Reference: Donald E. Miskiman, "The Treatment of Insomnia by the Technique of Transcendental Meditation" (University of Alberta, Edmonton, Alberta, Canada), *Scientific Research on the Transcendental Meditation Program: Collected Papers*, vol. 1, ed. David W. Orme-Johnson and John T. Farrow (New York: MIU Press, 1975).

CHART 5
Beneficial
Effects on
Bronchial
Asthma

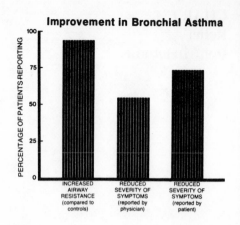

Improvement in Bronchial Asthma

PERCENTAGE OF PATIENTS REPORTING

INCREASED AIRWAY RESISTANCE (compared to controls)

REDUCED SEVERITY OF SYMPTOMS (reported by physician)

REDUCED SEVERITY OF SYMPTOMS (reported by patient)

Finding: After beginning the practice of Transcendental Meditation 94 percent of a group of asthmatic patients showed improvement as determined by the physiological measurement of airway resistance. Fifty-one percent of the asthmatic patients showed improvement as reported by their personal physicians, and 74 percent showed improvement as reported by the patients.

Interpretation: These results indicate that the Transcendental Meditation program is beneficial for patients with bronchial asthma. Bronchial asthma is one of a group of diseases whose severity has been consistently correlated with the level of psychological stress of the individual. By systematically relieving stress, Transcendental Meditation promises to be an effective new therapy for this and other psychosomatic diseases.

First reference: Ron Honsberger and Archie F. Wilson, "The Effect of Transcendental Meditation upon Bronchial Asthma," *Clinical Research* 2, no. 2 (1973). Reprinted in *Scientific Research on the Transcendental Meditation Program: Collected Papers*, vol. 1, ed. David W. Orme-Johnson and John T. Farrow (New York: MIU Press, 1975).

Second reference: Ron Honsberger and Archie F. Wilson, "Transcendental Meditation in Treating Asthma," *Respiratory Therapy: The Journal of Inhalation Technology* 3, no. 6 (1973): 79–81. Reprinted in *Scientific Research on the Transcendental Meditation Program: Collected Papers*, vol. 1, ed. David W. Orme-Johnson and John T. Farrow (New York: MIU Press, 1975).

Third reference: Archie F. Wilson, Ron Honsberger, J. T. Chinu, and H. S. Novey, "Transcendental Meditation and Asthma," *Respiration* (in press).

Fourth reference: Paul W. Corey, "Airway Conductance and Oxygen Consumption Changes Due to the Transcendental Meditation Technique" (University of Colorado Medical Center, Denver, Colorado), *Scientific Research on the Transcendental Meditation Program: Collected Papers*, vol. 1, ed. David W. Orme-Johnson and John T. Farrow (New York: MIU Press, 1975).

CHART 6
Faster
Reactions

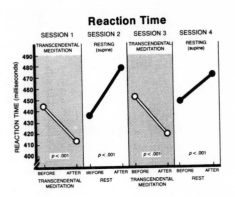

Reaction Time

SESSION 1 — TRANSCENDENTAL MEDITATION
SESSION 2 — RESTING (supine)
SESSION 3 — TRANSCENDENTAL MEDITATION
SESSION 4 — RESTING (supine)

REACTION TIME (milliseconds)

p < .001   p < .001   p < .001   p < .001

BEFORE AFTER — TRANSCENDENTAL MEDITATION
BEFORE AFTER — REST
BEFORE AFTER — TRANSCENDENTAL MEDITATION
BEFORE AFTER — REST

Finding: Transcendental Meditation was found to speed up reactions as compared with resting in a supine position, which resulted in a slowing of reactions. Twenty-five subjects were measured over four different sessions, and the effect of Transcendental Meditation in improving reaction time was consistent.

Interpretation: Transcendental Meditation speeds up reactions, indicating increased alertness, improved coordination of mind and body, and improved efficiency in perception and performance. This experiment also shows that TM results in significantly more freshness and alertness than is achieved by merely lying down. The state induced by the TM technique is a new and superior form of coherent deep rest.

First reference: David W. Orme-Johnson, David Kolb, and J. Russell Hebert, "An Experimental Analysis of the Effects of Transcendental Meditation," *Scientific Research on the Transcendental Meditation Program: Collected Papers*, vol. 1, ed. David W. Orme-Johnson and John T. Farrow (New York: MIU Press, 1975).

Second reference: Robert Shaw and David Kolb, "Improved Reaction Time Following the Transcendental Meditation Technique" (University of Texas, Austin), *Scientific Research on the Transcendental Meditation Program: Collected Papers*, vol. 1, ed. David W. Orme-Johnson and John T. Farrow (New York: MIU Press, 1975).

CHART 7
Superior Perceptual-Motor Performance

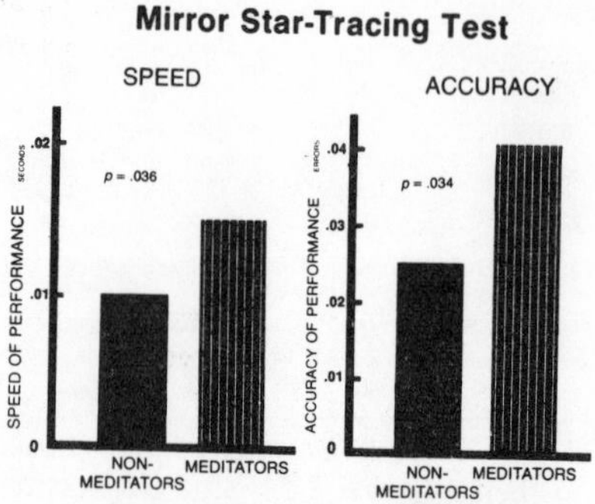

Mirror Star-Tracing Test

Finding: Subjects who were practicing Transcendental Meditation performed faster and more accurately on a complex perceptual-motor test (Mirror Star-Tracing Test). The test measures the ability to trace a pattern while watching its reflection in a mirror without becoming disoriented.

Interpretation: Performance as measured by this test is relevant to such tasks as driving a car, hitting a target, and performing in many different sports. The superior performance of meditators indicates that the Transcendental Meditation program brings greater coordination between mind and body, greater flexibility, increased perceptual awareness, superior resistance to disorientation, greater efficiency, and improved neuromuscular integration.

Reference: Karen S. Blasdell, "The Effects of the Transcendental Meditation Technique upon a Complex Perceptual-Motor Task" (University of California at Los Angeles), *Scientific Research on the Transcendental Meditation Program: Collected Papers*, vol. 1, ed. David W. Orme-Johnson and John T. Farrow (New York: MIU Press, 1975).

CHART 8
Broader
Comprehension
and Improved
Ability to
Focus Attention

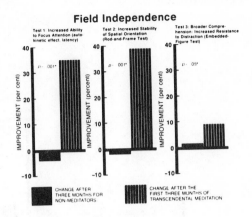

Field Independence

Finding: In this study three tests were administered that directly measure field independence, the ability to focus attention on specific objects without being distracted by the environment of the objects. Meditators changed significantly in the direction of increased field independence after practicing the Transcendental Meditation technique for three months, compared with a nonmeditating control group.

The latency of the autokinetic effect measures the ability to perceive the movement of a spot of light; the Rod-and-Frame Test measures the ability to orient a rod to true vertical against a tilted frame; and the Embedded-Figures Test measures the ability to perceive simple figures embedded in a complex background.

Interpretation: Increased field independence is known by psychologists to be associated with increased mental health, reduced anxiety, and increased stability of the autonomic nervous system—all indications of improved neurological organization and, consequently, more evolved consciousness. This improvement in meditators is remarkable because it was previously believed that these basic perceptual abilities do not improve beyond early adulthood.

Reference: Kenneth R. Pelletier, "Increased Perceptual Acuity Following Transcendental Meditation (University of California School of Medicine, San Francisco), *Scientific Research on the Transcendental Meditation Program: Collected Papers*, vol. 1, ed. David W. Orme-Johnson and John T. Farrow (New York: MIU Press, 1975).

CHART 9
Increased Intelligence Growth Rate

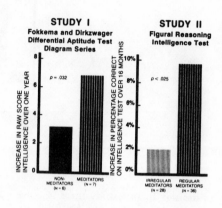

STUDY I
Fokkema and Dirkzwager
Differential Aptitude Test
Diagram Series

INCREASE IN RAW SCORE INTELLIGENCE OVER ONE YEAR

p = .032

NON-MEDITATORS (N = 6)   MEDITATORS (N = 7)

STUDY II
Figural Reasoning Intelligence Test

INCREASE IN PERCENTAGE CORRECT ON INTELLIGENCE TEST OVER 16 MONTHS

p < .025

IRREGULAR MEDITATORS (N = 28)   REGULAR MEDITATORS (N = 36)

Finding: The results of an initial study showed greater increases in intelligence among meditating high school students than among non-meditating controls. These results were confirmed in a second study that indicated that a group of university students and adults who practiced the Transcendental Meditation technique regularly (N = 36) increased significantly more in intelligence than those who did not meditate regularly (N = 28) over the 16-month period after they began Transcendental Meditation (p < .025).

Interpretation: These findings indicate that the Transcendental Meditation program increases general fluid intelligence, which enables the meditator to respond to new situations with greater adaptability, creativity, and comprehension. After the age when intelligence growth is expected to reach a plateau, meditators continue to grow.

Reference: André S. Tjoa, "Some Evidence That the Transcendental Meditation Program Increases Intelligence as Measured by a Psychological Test" (University of Leiden, Leiden, Holland), *Scientific Research on the Transcendental Meditation Program: Collected Papers*, vol. 1, ed. David W. Orme-Johnson and John T. Farrow (New York: MIU Press, 1975).

CHART 10
Increased Learning Ability

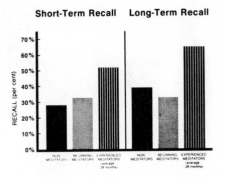

Short-Term Recall   **Long-Term Recall**

RECALL (per cent)

70%
60%
50%
40%
30%
20%
10%
0%

NON MEDITATORS | BEGINNING MEDITATORS | EXPERIENCED MEDITATORS (average 28 months) | NON MEDITATORS | BEGINNING MEDITATORS | EXPERIENCED MEDITATORS (average 28 months)

Finding: Subjects who had practiced the Transcendental Meditation technique an average of 28 months performed better than beginning meditators on short- and long-term recall tests as well as tests of paired-associate learning. Also, a trend toward progressive improvement in long-term recall was found in comparing nonmeditators, beginning meditators, and experienced meditators.

Interpretation: These results indicate that Transcendental Meditation directly improves the ability to learn. This finding is even more significant in view of the common belief among psychologists that basic learning ability cannot be improved beyond late adolescence.

Reference: Allan I. Abrams, "Paired-Associate Learning and Recall: A Pilot Study of the Transcendental Meditation Technique" (University of California at Berkeley), *Scientific Research on the Transcendental Meditation Program: Collected Papers*, vol. 1, ed. David W. Orme-Johnson and John T. Farrow (New York: MIU Press, 1975).

CHART 11
Increased
Orderliness
of Thinking I

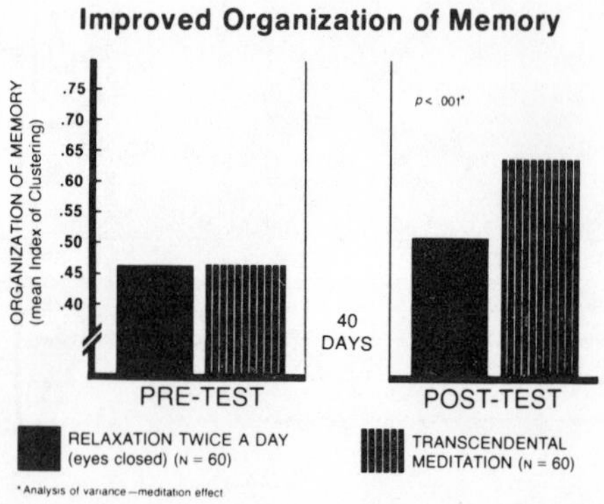

Improved Organization of Memory

ORGANIZATION OF MEMORY
(mean Index of Clustering)

.75
.70
.65
.60
.55
.50
.45
.40

$p < .001^*$

40
DAYS

PRE-TEST

POST-TEST

RELAXATION TWICE A DAY
(eyes closed) (N = 60)

TRANSCENDENTAL
MEDITATION (N = 60)

* Analysis of variance—meditation effect

Finding: After the first 40 days of the Transcendental Meditation program, meditators increased markedly in their tendency to spontaneously organize memorized material in their minds (as measured by the Index of Clustering in recall); members of the control group, who relaxed twice daily by sitting with the eyes closed, did not change significantly.

Interpretation: This study shows one aspect of the basic tendency of Transcendental Meditation to improve the orderliness of the mind. The ability of TM to systematically develop clarity of thought demonstrates that the associated neurophysiological changes, such as increased balance of the cerebral hemispheres [see Figure 1, p. 29], are in a highly desirable direction.

Reference: Donald E. Miskiman, "The Effect of the Transcendental Meditation Technique on the Organization of Thinking and Recall (Secondary Organization)" (University of Alberta, Edmonton, Alberta, Canada), *Scientific Research on the Transcendental Meditation Program: Collected Papers*, vol. 1, ed. David W. Orme-Johnson and John T. Farrow (New York: MIU Press, 1975).

CHART 12
Increased
Orderliness
of Thinking II

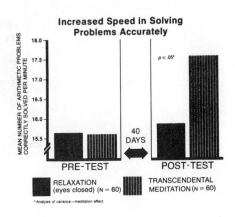

Increased Speed in Solving Problems Accurately

MEAN NUMBER OF ARITHMETIC PROBLEMS CORRECTLY SOLVED PER MINUTE

18.0
17.5
17.0
16.5
16.0
15.5

$p < .05^*$

40 DAYS

PRE-TEST   POST-TEST

■ RELAXATION (eyes closed) (N = 60)   ▨ TRANSCENDENTAL MEDITATION (N = 60)

* Analysis of variance—meditation effect.

Finding: After beginning the Transcendental Meditation technique, meditators significantly increased their speed in solving arithmetic problems accurately. Two facts were found:

1. The efficiency of solving the arithmetic problems increased in meditators compared with members of a control group who relaxed for an equivalent period twice daily.
2. A separate test of memory (Chart 11) showed that improved organization of memory took place even while the meditators were engaged in problem solving.

Interpretation: These results show that Transcendental Meditation increases the clarity and efficiency of conscious thought processes and at the same time improves the unconscious processes leading to spontaneous and purposeful organization of thought. . . .

Reference: Donald E. Miskiman, "The Effect of the Transcendental Meditation Technique on the Organization of Thinking and Recall (Secondary Organization)" (University of Alberta, Edmonton, Alberta, Canada), *Scientific Research on the Transcendental Meditation Program: Collected Papers*, vol. 1, ed. David W. Orme-Johnson and John T. Farrow (New York: MIU Press, 1975).

CHART 13
Increased
Orderliness
of Thinking III

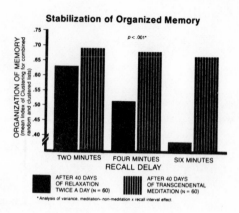

Stabilization of Organized Memory

Finding: The organization of memory in meditators was stronger and more stable over time than in control subjects. The comparison was between two groups: One group of 60 subjects had relaxed for an equivalent period twice a day. Over a two- to six-month interval, the meditators' memories decreased only 3 percent in efficiency of recall while the non-meditators' memories decreased 38 percent.

Interpretation: This indicates an increased clarity and stability of mind in those who practice the Transcendental Meditation technique. Whereas Transcendental Meditation produced increased orderliness of thinking and remembering, ordinary relaxation with eyes closed had little effect (see also Charts 11 and 12).

Taken together with the finding that Transcendental Meditation produces more orderly brain functioning than does ordinary relaxation, these results indicate that Transcendental Meditation is different from and superior to ordinary relaxation. TM is a new technology with profound implications for developing a more orderly physiology and psychology.

Reference: Donald E. Miskiman, "The Effect of the Transcendental Meditation Technique on the Organization of Thinking and Recall (Secondary Organization)" (University of Alberta, Edmonton, Alberta, Canada), *Scientific Research on the Transcendental Meditation Program: Collected Papers*, vol. 1, ed. David W. Orme-Johnson and John T. Farrow (New York: MIU Press, 1975).

CHART 14
Increased Intellectual Performance in High School Students

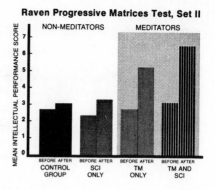

Raven Progressive Matrices Test, Set II

Finding: This study involved 80 students in a Canadian public high school. Intellectual performance was measured by the Raven Progressive Matrices Test, Set II, before and after a 14-week Transcendental Meditation program. The meditating students' scores showed significantly greater gains in intellectual ability than did the nonmeditators scores. Also, it was shown that gains in intellectual ability were due primarily to the experience of the Transcendental Meditation technique itself, not simply to intellectual involvement with the theory underlying it, as presented in an accompanying Science of Creative Intelligence course. Students who did take the SCI course were more regular in their practice of Transcendental Meditation and scored even higher on this measure.

Interpretation: The introduction of the Transcendental Meditation and the Science of Creative Intelligence program into secondary education promises a unique advance in the effectiveness of the entire high school curriculum. Whereas all other courses in the secondary school offer knowledge, the Transcendental Meditation technique, which is the practical, experiential aspect of the Science of Creative Intelligence, offers [a] . . . natural means to expand the container of knowledge, the consciousness of the student, as shown by increased intellectual performance. This aspect of neurophysiological education is complemented by the Science of Creative Intelligence course, which allows the student to understand intellectually the basis of his newfound clear thinking and accelerated progress. . . .

First reference: Howard Shecter, "The Transcendental Meditation Program in the Classroom: A Psychological Evaluation of the Science of Creative Intelligence" (York University, North York, Ontario, Canada), *Scientific Research on the Transcendental Meditation Program: Collected Papers,* vol. 1, ed. David W. Orme-Johnson and John T. Farrow (New York: MIU Press, 1975).

Second reference: *Science of Creative Intelligence for Secondary Education* (New York: MIU Press, 1975).

CHART 15
Development
of Personality

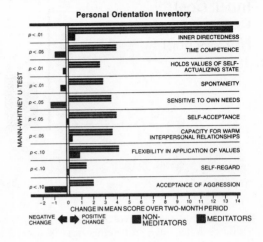

Personal Orientation Inventory

MANN-WHITNEY U TEST

p < .01	INNER DIRECTEDNESS
p < .05	TIME COMPETENCE
p < .01	HOLDS VALUES OF SELF-ACTUALIZING STATE
p < .01	SPONTANEITY
p < .05	SENSITIVE TO OWN NEEDS
p < .05	SELF-ACCEPTANCE
p < .05	CAPACITY FOR WARM INTERPERSONAL RELATIONSHIPS
p < .10	FLEXIBILITY IN APPLICATION OF VALUES
p < .10	SELF-REGARD
p < .10	ACCEPTANCE OF AGGRESSION

-2 -1 0 1 2 3 4 5 6 7 8 9 10 11 12 13 14
CHANGE IN MEAN SCORE OVER TWO-MONTH PERIOD
NEGATIVE CHANGE ← → POSITIVE CHANGE ■ NON-MEDITATORS ■ MEDITATORS

Finding: Subjects practicing Transcendental Meditation, measured once prior to beginning the technique and again two months later, showed significant positive improvement in the following traits when compared with a matched control group of nonmeditators: inner-directedness, time competence, self-actualization, spontaneity, sensitivity to one's needs, self-acceptance, and capacity for warm interpersonal relationships. The test used was the Personal Orientation Inventory (POI) developed by Shostram. Two independent studies also using the POI confirmed these results.

Interpretation: All the personality changes brought about by Transcendental Meditation are in the direction of what is generally recognized as the development of a healthy, self-actualized personality.

First reference: William Seeman, Sanford Nidich, and Thomas Banta, "Influence of Transcendental Meditation on a Measure of Self-Actualization," *Journal of Counseling Psychology* 19, no. 3 (1972): 184–187.

Second reference: Sanford Nidich, William Seeman, and Thomas Dreskin, "Influence of Transcendental Meditation: A Replication," *Journal of Counseling Psychology* 20, no. 6 (1973): 565–566. Reprinted in *Scientific Research on the Transcendental Meditation Program: Collected Papers*, vol. 1, ed. David W. Orme-Johnson and John T. Farrow (New York: MIU Press, 1975).

Third reference: Larry A. Hjelle, "Transcendental Meditation and Psychological Health," *Perceptual and Motor Skills* 39 (1974): 623–628. Reprinted in *Scientific Research on the Transcendental Meditation Program: Collected Papers*, vol. 1, ed. David W. Orme-Johnson and John T. Farrow (New York: MIU Press, 1975).

CHART 16
Increased
Inner Control,
Decreased
Anxiety

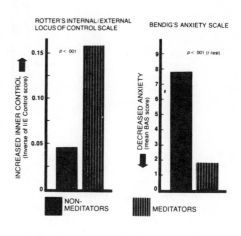

ROTTER'S INTERNAL/EXTERNAL
LOCUS OF CONTROL SCALE

BENDIG'S ANXIETY SCALE

Finding: Compared with a control group of nonmeditators, subjects practicing the Transcendental Meditation technique were significantly more internally controlled, as measured by Rotter's Locus of Control Scale, and were significantly less anxious, as measured by Bendig's Anxiety Scale.

Interpretation: In modern psychology high "internal locus of control" is considered a reliable index of overall personality adjustment and ability to learn from and deal effectively with complex situations. Since the TM technique stabilizes the internal sense of self and improves the integration and therefore the effectiveness of thought and action, the meditator feels a greater sense of control over his life.

Reference: Larry A. Hjelle, "Transcendental Meditation and Psychological Health." *Perceptual and Motor Skills* 39 (1974): 623–628. Reprinted in *Scientific Research on the Transcendental Meditation Program: Collected Papers*, vol. 1, ed. David W. Orme-Johnson and John T. Farrow (New York: MIU Press, 1975).

CHART 17
Increased
Energy Level in
High School
Students

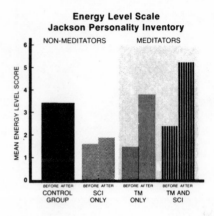

Energy Level Scale
Jackson Personality Inventory

Finding: In a study involving 80 students in a Canadian public high school, students who practiced Transcendental Meditation showed a significant increase in energy level ($p < .001$) after 14 weeks of the TM program, as measured by the Jackson Personality Inventory, whereas the control group showed no change. Also, it was shown that increased energy level was primarily due to the experience of the TM technique itself, and not simply to intellectual involvement with the theory underlying it, as presented in an accompanying Science of Creative Intelligence course. Participation in the SCI course was reported to improve regularity of the practice of TM.

Interpretation: Improved psychological energy level in any individual is the consequence of better physiological and neurophysiological functioning, which leads to finer perceptions and faster reactions (see Charts 6–8). Whereas dullness and lack of interest are a problem in many high school classes, students practicing Transcendental Meditation are likely to become sharper, brighter, and livelier.

Reference: Howard Shecter, "The Transcendental Meditation Program in the Classroom: A Psychological Evaluation of the Science of Creative Intelligence" (York University, North York, Ontario, Canada), *Scientific Research on the Transcendental Meditation Program: Collected Papers*, vol. 1, ed. David W. Orme-Johnson and John T. Farrow (New York: MIU Press, 1975).

CHART 18
Increased Creativity

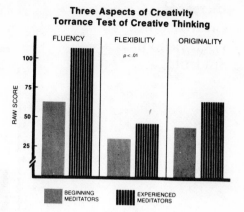

Three Aspects of Creativity
Torrance Test of Creative Thinking

FLUENCY   FLEXIBILITY   ORIGINALITY

p < .01

RAW SCORE

100
75
50
25

BEGINNING MEDITATORS   EXPERIENCED MEDITATORS

Finding: The Torrance Test of Creative Thinking (TTCT), Verbal Form A, was used to compare 44 subjects practicing the Transcendental Meditation technique for several months with 41 subjects who had just learned Transcendental Meditation. The two groups were equivalent in age, sex, education, and income level. The experienced meditators scored significantly higher ($p < 0.01$) on all three scales of the TTCT—Fluency, Flexibility, and Originality—indicating that the practice of Transcendental Meditation increases creativity.

Interpretation: The TTCT was developed to measure the type of creative thinking process described by eminent scientific researchers, inventors, and creative writers. Psychologists such as Carl Rogers and Abraham Maslow have associated this type of creativity with increased self-actualization, which has also been found to result from Transcendental Meditation in independent studies (for example, Phillip C. Ferguson and John C. Gowan, "Psychological Findings on Transcendental Meditation," paper presented to the California State Psychological Association, Fresno, California, 1974, *Journal of Humanistic Psychology*, in press). These findings give objective validation to the statement that Transcendental Meditation systematically develops creative intelligence by providing a means to directly experience the source of creativity in the mind. The aspects of creativity measured here—fluency, flexibility, and originality—may be associated with integration, adaptability, and growth. . . .

Reference: Michael J. MacCallum, "Transcendental Meditation and Creativity" (California State University at Long Beach), *Scientific Research on the Transcendental Meditation Program: Collected Papers*, vol. 1, ed. David W. Orme-Johnson and John T. Farrow (New York: MIU Press, 1975).

CHART 19
Increased Creativity in High School Students

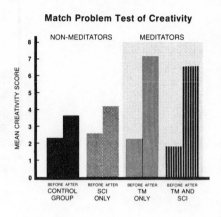

Match Problem Test of Creativity

Finding: This study involved 80 students in a Canadian public high school. Creativity was measured by the Match Problem Test before and after a 14-week Transcendental Meditation program. The meditating students' scores showed significantly greater gains in creativity than the nonmeditating students' scores. Also, it was shown that gains in creativity were primarily due to the practice of the Transcendental Meditation technique itself, not simply to intellectual involvement with the theory underlying it, as presented in an accompanying Science of Creative Intelligence course. Participation in the Science of Creative Intelligence course was reported to improve regularity of practice of Transcendental Meditation.

Interpretation: Greater creativity is the product of a more lively and integrated nervous system. What Transcendental Meditation adds to secondary education is the opportunity for the student to establish a habit early in life of preparing for fruitful activity by engaging in a systematic procedure to contact the source of creative thought within himself. A more creative high school graduate means a more productive and fulfilled citizen. The implication of this study is that the addition of Transcendental Meditation to the secondary school curriculum represents a major advance in the effectiveness of high school education.

Reference: Howard Shecter, "The Transcendental Meditation Program in the Classroom: A Psychological Evaluation of the Science of Creative Intelligence (York University, North York, Ontario, Canada), *Scientific Research on the Transcendental Meditation Program: Collected Papers*, vol. 1, ed. David W. Orme-Johnson and John T. Farrow (New York: MIU Press, 1975).

CHART 20
Reduced
Drug Abuse

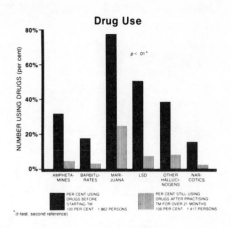

Drug Use

Finding: A retrospective study of 1,862 subjects who practiced Transcendental Meditation an average of 20 months showed decreases in the reported use of nonprescribed drugs. A longitudinal study of 76 drug users during the first year after they began Transcendental Meditation showed that 70 percent of the group had discontinued use of all drugs nine months after starting TM. Use of cannabis was reduced 58 percent, hallucinogens 91 percent, amphetamines 96 percent, and opiates 78 percent.

Interpretation: Because Transcendental Meditation has been shown to improve inner control and decrease anxiety (Chart 16) and to strengthen mental health and general well-being, it may be concluded that the desire for drugs is thereby decreased or eliminated. This study indicates that the Transcendental Meditation program may be the most effective antidote for drug abuse because its success does not depend on any initial resolve on the part of the subject to discontinue bad habits.

First reference: Herbert Benson and Robert Keith Wallace, "Decreased Drug Abuse with Transcendental Meditation: A Study of 1,862 Subjects," *Drug Abuse: Proceedings of the International Conference*, ed. Chris J. D. Zarafonetis (Philadelphia: Lea and Febiger, 1972): 369–376 and *Congressional Record*, Serial No. 92–1 (Washington, D.C.: U.S. Government Printing Office, 1971). Reprinted in *Scientific Research on the Transcendental Meditation Program: Collected Papers*, vol. 1, ed. David W. Orme-Johnson and John T. Farrow (New York: MIU Press, 1975).

Second reference: Mohammed Shafii, Richard A. Lavely, and Robert D. Jaffe, "Meditation and Marijuana," *American Journal of Psychiatry* 131, no. 1 (1974): 60–63. Reprinted in *Scientific Research on the Transcendental Meditation Program: Collected Papers*, vol. 1, ed. David W. Orme-Johnson and John T. Farrow (New York: MIU Press, 1975).

Recommended Readings

Argyris, C. *Interpersonal Competence and Organizational Effectiveness.* Homewood, Ill.: Irwin-Dorsey, 1962.

Banquet, J. P. "EEG and Meditation." *Electroencephalography and Clinical Neurophysiology,* Vol. 33, 1972, pp. 449–458.

——. "Spectral Analysis of the EEG in Meditation." *Electroencephalography and Clinical Neurophysiology,* Vol. 35, 1973, pp. 143–151.

Benson, H., and R. K. Wallace. "Decreased Blood Pressure in Hypertensive Subjects Who Practiced Meditation." Supplement II to *Circulation,* Vols. XLV and XLVI, October 1972. Abstracts of the 45th Scientific Sessions.

Blasdell, K. "The Effect of Transcendental Meditation Upon a Complex Perceptual Motor Test." *Scientific Research on Transcendental Meditation: Collected Papers,* edited by D. W. Orme-Johnson, L. H. Domash, and J. T. Farrow. Los Angeles: Maharishi International University Press, 1974.

Bloomfield, H., M. P. Cain, and D. T. Jaffe, with R. B. Kory. *TM: Discovering Inner Energy and Overcoming Stress.* New York: Delacorte Press, 1975.

"Business Turns on to TM," *Connecticut Business and Industry,* December 1974.

Christopher, William F. *The Achieving Enterprise.* New York: AMACOM, 1974.

Domash, L. "Physics and the Study of Consciousness: Does Transcendental Meditation Induce a Macroscopic Quantum State in the Nervous System?" Department of Physics, Maharishi International University, Santa Barbara, Calif., 1974.

Fenton, M. "Transcendental Meditation: A Novitiate's Report." *Managers' Forum*, Vol. 2, No. 2, February 1975.

Forem, J. *Transcendental Meditation, Maharishi Mahesh Yogi and the Science of Creative Intelligence*. New York: E. P. Dutton & Company, 1973.

Frew, D. R. "Transcendental Meditation and Productivity." *Academy of Management Journal*, Vol. 17, No. 2, June 1974.

—— "Unstressing the Stressed-up Executive." *Conference Board Record*, July 1975.

Glueck, B. C., and C. S. Stroebel. "The Psychobiology of Transcendental Meditation." *Current Psychiatric Therapies*. New York: Grune & Stratton, 1975.

Herzberg, F. *Work and the Nature of Man*. New York: New American Library, 1973.

James, W. *William James on Psychical Research*. Edited by G. Murphy and R. V. Ballou. New York: Viking Press, 1963.

Jones, M., and V. Mellersh. "Comparison of Exercise Response in Anxiety States and Normal Controls." *Psychosomatic Medicine*, Vol. 8, 1946, pp. 180–187.

Kanellakos, D. P., and J. S. Lukas. *The Psychobiology of Transcendental Meditation: Literature Survey*. Reading, Pa.: W. A. Benjamin Co., 1974.

Kleitman, N. *Sleep and Wakefulness*. Revised and enlarged ed. Chicago: University of Chicago Press, 1963.

Levi, L., ed. *Stress: Sources, Management, and Prevention*. New York: Liveright Publishing Corp., 1967.

Maharishi Mahesh Yogi. *The Science of Being and the Art of Living*. Stuttgart, Germany: Spiritual Regeneration Movement Publications, 1966.

Marrow, A. J., ed. *The Failure of Success*. New York: AMACOM, 1972.

Maslow, A. H. "Theory Z." *Journal of Transpersonal Psychology*. Fall 1969, pp. 31–47.

——. *Toward a Psychology of Being*. New York: D. Van Nostrand Co., 1968.

Nidich, S., W. Seeman, and T. Dreskin. "Influence of Transcendental Meditation: A Replication." *Journal of Counseling Psychology*, 20, No. 6, 1973, pp. 565-566.

Orme-Johnson, D. W. "Autonomic Stability and Transcendental Meditation." *Psychosomatic Medicine*, Vol. 35, No. 4, July–August 1973, pp. 341-349.

Penfield, W., and T. Rasmussen. *The Cerebral Cortex of Man: A Clinical Study of Localization of Function*. New York: Macmillan, 1950.

Perls, F. S. *Gestalt Therapy Verbatim*. LaFayette, Calif.: Real People Press, 1969.

"Personal Business," *Business Week*, October 26, 1974.

Scientific Research on Transcendental Meditation: Collected Papers, Vol. 1. Edited by D. W. Orme-Johnson, L. H. Domash, and J. T. Farrow. New York: Maharishi International University Press, 1975.

Wallace, R. K. "Physiological Effects of Transcendental Meditation." *Science*, Vol. 167, March 27, 1970, pp. 1751–1754.

Wallace, R. K., and H. Benson. "Physiological Effects of a Meditation Technique and a Suggestion for Curbing Drug Abuse." Mental Health Program Reports, Thorndike Memorial Laboratory, Harvard University School of Medicine, December 5, 1971.

Wilson, A. F., and R. Honsberger. "The Effects of Transcendental Meditation upon Bronchial Asthma." *Clinical Research*, Vol. 2, No. 2, 1973.

Woolridge, D. E. *The Machinery of the Brain*. New York: McGraw-Hill, 1966.